Using Records of
Achievement in
Higher Education

Using Records of Achievement in Higher Education

EDITED BY
Alison Assiter and Eileen Shaw

**KOGAN
PAGE**

London • Philadelphia

First published in 1993

Kogan Page Limited
120 Pentonville Road
London N1 9JN

British Library Cataloguing in Publication Data

A CIP record for this book is available from the British Library.
ISBN 0 7494 1111 2

Typeset by Saxon Graphics Ltd, Derby

Printed and bound in Great Britain by Biddles Ltd, Guildford and King's Lynn

Contents

6

Acknowledgements

We would like to thank the following people and organizations for their help in putting this book together:

Higher Education for Capability, for presenting the 'Using Records of Achievement' conference from which much of the material has been drawn; Enterprise In Higher Education at the Leeds Metropolitan University, Enterprise In Higher Education at the University of Leeds and the Recording Achievement and Higher Education project at Wigan for their support for the conference;

Val Butcher, Allan Hardy and Rob Ward for helping to plan the conference programme;

Helen Pearson, Naomi Wilds and Rachel Green for organizing the conference;

Woolley Hall, Wakefield for hosting the conference;

David Pierce of the Employment Department for his support for the production of the book;

Lisa Joynes of Higher Education for Capability for providing administrative support for the preparation of the manuscript.

The Contributors

Alison Assiter is EHE programme manager at the University of North London. Recently she spent a year at the CNAA, working on a national project in HE on profiling and recording achievement, and she is one of the co-authors (with Angela Fenwick *et al.*) of *Profiling in HE* (CNAA and TEED, 1992). Prior to that she taught philosophy/humanities for many years at Thames Polytechnic (now the University of Greenwich). Her previous publications include *Pornography, Feminism and the Individual* (Pluto Press, 1989), *Althusser and Feminism* (Pluto Press, 1990) and *Bad Girls; Dirty Pictures* (ed., with Avedon Carol, Pluto Press, 1993).

Robert J Bellis is senior graduate recruitment manager, KPMG Peat Marwick. Qualifying as a chartered accountant in 1979, Robert spent eight years working with clients in Edinburgh, Cambridge and London, becoming more and more involved in recruitment and training. In 1987 he moved full time into graduate recruitment and is now in charge of the London office intake of some 150 graduates and helps coordinate KPMG's national programme. He is also an executive member of AGR (the Association of Graduate Recruiters) and involved with EHE programmes in a number of institutions.

Karen M Carter is lecturer in drama (initial teacher education) and education management (in-service education) at the Didsbury School of Education, Manchester Metropolitan University. She is BEd. (Hons) course development officer with responsibility for reporting systems and recording achievement initiatives and 'RoA in HE Project' evaluator, involving work with schools, LEAs and HE institutions. Previously she was a primary school teacher for Manchester LEA, involved in developmental work on profiling.

Lesley Cooke is currently assistant dean of academic studies at Chester College. Working in the college and community as a chartered psychologist and partaking in study visits to Alverno College, Milwaukee, USA, have offered her opportunities to explore her interest in the role of action learning in student development. She is currently involved in developments within work-based learning, action learning and the implementation of Records of Achievement within higher education.

Katherine Cuthbert lectures in psychology at the Crewe and Alsager Faculty of Manchester Metropolitan University. She teaches on a BA in applied social studies, an innovative degree within which students complete a major final year project, counting for up to 80 per cent of the final year assessment. She has a long-standing interest in student learning, particularly the promotion of students' intellectual and personal skills.

Sue Drew is a senior lecturer in the department of development services at Sheffield Hallam University, working with staff to encourage approaches which foster the personal and professional development of students.

David Eaton is acting director, and **Chris Short** is a senior lecturer in the School of Engineering, Sheffield City Polytechnic; both have been closely involved in planning and implementing portfolio assessment and the Professional and Personal Development Programme which supports it.

Angela Fenwick is currently a research fellow at the Open University working on a project investigating approaches to the development of students' subject area knowledge and skills in the workplace and the necessary provision of learning support. She previously worked for CNAA on a project entitled 'Profiling work-based learning in academic courses' and is the joint author of a series of 1992 CNAA publications on profiling: *Profiling in HE: Guidelines to the development and use of profiling schemes; Profiling work-based learning in academic courses; briefing paper No. 32; Profiling and the assessment of work-based learning: an annotated bibliography.*

Howard Foster is director of enterprise in higher education at the University of Huddersfield and spent ten years in industry, latterly as manager of Dowty Electronic Systems Division, before joining the University as a lecturer in engineering. He has directed the University's EHE programme from the beginning. He is shortly to leave the university to work as an independent management consultant in education and training.

Jane Lynda Fox is principal of the College of Nursing and Midwifery which is in the Institute of Health and Community Studies of Derbyshire College of Higher Education.

Helen Gladstone took a first degree in the humanities through the Open University and continued at the Open University with interdisciplinary research for a doctorate. During the past three years she has worked for the Enterprise Initiative Unit at Brunel University to bring about changes in teaching practices and in the assessment of students' workplace experiences.

Joyce Godfrey is currently Record of Achievement manager at the University of Sheffield. Over the past six months she has continued with her development of a generic ROA profile. She is also working with the university medical school to develop a ROA containing a profile of clinical skills. She has several years experience teaching in HE and FE and has been involved in curriculum development of competency based Cert. Ed. (FE) courses, including profiles of professional skills and RoAs. She is chief external examiner to the Cert Ed./PGCE course at Greenwich University. Prior to the above she spent 17 years in different professional roles within the NHS.

Roy Gregory is a principal lecturer at the University of Hertfordshire. He is currently scheme tutor for MEng in the Engineering Programme. He is enterprise tutor for the School of Engineering with responsibility for the developments in teaching and learning, group skills, and the teaching of personal transferable skills. He has developed packages for self development and profiling for undergraduates.

Richard Gretton now works freelance in assessment, recording and reporting of achievement with HE institutions, schools, colleges and LEAs. Formerly, he was a senior research fellow at the University of Sussex on the Admissions to HE project, which investigates the role of selection criteria and Records of Achievement in the admissions process. He worked on the South-East Record of Achievement (SERA) scheme between 1985 and 1990, having previously taught in Kent for eight years.

Roger Harrison is a lecturer with the School of Education at the Open University. He has worked on a range of courses relating to adult life transitions, and is currently chair of the materials development team for the OU's EHE programme.

Heather Hughes Jones is head of marketing and external relations at the Bolton Institute. She is actively concerned with furthering the Institute's mission to widen participation in higher education and she chairs the Institute's working group on access and continuing education. As well as the 'Passport' scheme for local youngsters, she also organizes a range of link activities with the community to encourage access for women returners, ethnic minorities and the unemployed. Heather has been at the Bolton Institute for three years and has been active in continuing education and continuing professional development for ten years.

Ros McCulloch is co-director of the Centre for English, School of Education, Leicester University and is also a PGCE tutor. She has published widely in the areas of student entitlement and flexible learning techniques. She is currently writing and trialling interactive student guides in study skills and subject-specific areas in Leicester, Nottingham and De Montfort Universities, and working with postgraduate students on effective thesis-writing techniques.

Daniel Moy is a graduate of Dublin and Manchester Universities. His career in education, training and people development spans over 30 years, and includes experience in schools, the RAF and two major UK retailing companies. He currently runs his own consultancy business. Mr Moy served as a CBI representative on the National Steering Committee for Records of Achievement.

Lovemore Nyatanga is vice-principal of the College of Nursing and Midwifery which is in the Institute of Health and Community Studies of Derbyshire College of Higher Education.

Roger Payne is a senior lecturer in the department of Development Services,

Sheffield Hallam University, working with staff on aspects of courses which support students' personal and professional development.

Keith Selkirk taught mathematics in secondary schools for 11 years until 1971 when he became a lecturer (later senior lecturer) at the University of Nottingham, where he also obtained his PhD. His major interests in education are in mathematics education, educational assessment, Records of Achievement and research in education.

Eileen Shaw is a senior lecturer in education in the Faculty of Cultural and Education Studies, Leeds Metropolitan University. She has been heavily involved in developing Records of Achievement regionally and nationally for some 20 years in schools and more recently in higher education, through Enterprise in Higher Education and Higher Education for Capability. She was awarded the degree of Doctor of Philosophy by the University of Leeds in 1991 for her thesis *Records of Achievement in the North of England: 1983–1990*.

Nigel Smalls is the training manager at Courtaulds Textiles plc. After seven years in operational roles, Nigel has spent the last two years helping to develop a competency model for managers, and selling the idea within the company for use in selection and training and development.

Beryl Susan Starr is currently working at the University of Hertfordshire as Principal Lecturer in Psychology. She has been scheme leader for the BSc. honours psychology degree at the university for the last five years.

Maggie Taylor joined Chester College as enterprise manager in May 1990. This appointment followed a career in personnel management in the manufacturing industry, and teaching and management consultancy in higher education institutes committed to work-based and action learning.

Lin Thorley is currently enterprise director at the University of Hertfordshire. She has been in education most of her working life, initially teaching biology then moving into the humanities. The move convinced her of the importance of learning skills, and now she works as a practitioner in the development of personal skills and student-centred learning methods.

Marilyn Wedgewood, director of the University of Sheffield's regional office, previously lectured in biological sciences at Manchester Polytechnic. She became involved with BTEC as a course leader, moderator and adviser and developed an interest in monitoring students' learning. From a secondment to EHE at Manchester Polytechnic she became the EHE director at the University of Sheffield where an RoA was developed as part of the EHE programme and where she also served on Sheffield's Record of Achievement and experience validations board. She has talked and written on the subject of RoAs.

Keith Willis is currently the industrial placement manager for the School of Construction at Sheffield Hallam University.

Glossary

AGCAS	Association of Graduate Careers Advisory Services
AMI	American Management Institute
APEL	Assessment of Prior Experiential Learning
APL	Accreditation of Prior Learning
BA	Bachelor of Arts
BSc	Bachelor of Science
BEd	Bachelor of Education
BEng	Bachelor of Engineering
BTEC	Business and Technology Education Council
CATS	Credit Accumulation and Transfer Scheme
CCDU	Careers Counselling and Development Unit
CNAA	Council for National Academic Awards
CV	Curriculum Vitae
DES	Department of Education and Science (now Department for Education)
DES & WO	Department of Education and Science and the Welsh Office
EHE	Enterprise in Higher Education
FE	Further Education
GCE A	General Certificate of Education – Advanced Level
GCE O	General Certificate of Education – Ordinary Level
GCSE	General Certificate of Secondary Education
GNVQ	General National Vocational Qualification
HE	Higher Education
HEI	Higher Education Institution
HEC	Higher Education for Capability
HMSO	Her Majesty's Stationery Office
HND	Higher National Diploma
HPD	High Performance Development
ICAEW	Institute of Chartered Accountants in England and Wales
ICE	Institute of Civil Engineers
ICAS	Institute of Chartered Accountants in Scotland
KPMG	Klynveld Peat Marwick Goerdeller

LA	Local Authority
LEA	Local Education Authority
MCI	Management Charter Initiative
MYEC	Make Your Experience Count
NCVQ	National Council for Vocational Qualifications
NICEC	National Institute for Careers Education and Counselling
NRA	National Record of Achievement
NROVA	National Record of Vocational Achievement
PCAS	Polytechnics Central Admissions System
PDP	Personal Development Plan
PGCE	Postgraduate Certificate in Education
PPD	Personal and Professional Development
PSQ	Personal Skills and Qualities
RANSC	Records of Achievement National Steering Committee
ROA	Record of Achievement
RSA	Royal Society for the Encouragement of Arts Manufactures and Commerce
SCOTVEC	Scottish Vocational Education Council
TVE	Technical and Vocational Education
TVEI	Technical and Vocational Education Initiative
UCCA	University Central Council on Admissions
VSO	Voluntary Service Overseas

Preface

Interest in Records of Achievement is high in all sectors of education. Initially this interest was in part an acknowledgement of the limitations of conventional examination certificates in doing justice to the full range of learning achieved by students, and in part a response to the needs of employers for more detailed information about the abilities and interests of applicants for employment. More recently, interest has focused on the educational value to students of the experience of monitoring, reviewing and recording their own learning both inside and outside their school, college or university courses. Common cause has been established with a number of enlightened employers whose staff development procedures involve employees in joint appraisals of their own development.

Following the introduction of the National Record of Achievement (NRA) by the government during the late eighties, the preparation of Records of Achievement is a regular feature of the work of students and teachers in schools and colleges. Universities have begun to consider their relevance to the selection of students and to devise procedures for accommodating the greater range of information on each applicant which these records provide. Universities are also finding that Records of Achievement can be useful when considering the increasing number of applications from older students wishing to enter higher education without formal educational qualifications.

Involving students and employees in monitoring, reviewing and recording their own learning and experience is consistent with the growing emphasis being placed by both educators and employers on the development of autonomy in learning. Rapidly changing circumstances at work and in society are putting a premium on adaptability, working together and learning from experience. In the UK, national movements such as Higher Education for Capability (an initiative of the Royal Society for the encouragement of Arts, Manufactures and Commerce (RSA) based in Leeds Metropolitan University and the University of Leeds) and the Department of Employment's Enterprise in Higher Education initiative have stimulated much interesting experiment and innovation.

The material presented in this book is drawn from the experience of more than 200 people who attended the 'Using Records of Achievement' conference organized in July 1992 by Higher Education for Capability in association with the Enterprise in Higher Education projects of the Leeds Metropolitan University and the University of Leeds and the Recording Achievement and Higher Education project based in Wigan. The participants included people with experience of using Records of Achievement in schools, colleges, universities and large companies.

We begin in Part One with an overview of the general features of the recording achievement movement. The experience reported in Part Two is divided into five sections, each focused on a distinctive theme. The sequence of themes reflects our view that creating and managing records should be seen as a continuous activity covering transition from school and college to higher education (Section 1) through university itself (Sections 2, 3 and 4) and into employment (Section 5). Most of the experience relates to higher education which in turn is sub-divided into using records as a vehicle for empowering the learner (Section 2), using records as a means of developing a range of personal skills and qualities (Section 4) and issues related to assessment and accreditation. Part Three provides a review of this experience, including the issues raised, ways forward and the potential for further development.

This latest in the 'Using...' series of books will be of interest to all with responsibility for the design and delivery of the curriculum in higher and further education. We do not provide blue-prints or models of good practice but present glimpses of what others are doing and what they have learned from doing it, leaving readers to judge their relevance to their own circumstances. Higher Education for Capability (HEC) would like to hear of other examples, particularly where they may better illustrate some of the issues raised*. HEC publicizes examples in its National Capability and Enterprise Database (NCED) which is available internationally via the Joint Academic Computer Network. The 'Using...' series is intended to be the start of an exchange of experience which might ultimately lead to greater understanding of the processes of teaching and learning in higher and further education.

*Higher Education for Capability, 20 Queen Square, Leeds, LS2 8AF; telephone 0532 347725, facsimile 0532 442025.

Professor John Stephenson
Series Editor

Part One:
The Context

Chapter One

Records of Achievement: Background, Definitions and Uses

Alison Assiter and Eileen Shaw

Background and definitions

Background

What is a Record of Achievement or Profile? In order to respond to this question or attempt any firm definition, it is necessary to look at the historical context and rationale of the RoA movement.

The idea of secondary school pupils leaving school with a comprehensive report, or record of their achievement built up throughout their school careers, is not a new one. In 1943 the Norwood Committee advocated the introduction of a new form of school leaving certificate, but it was not until the 1970s that the schools started to make considerable use of RoAs. At this stage, the decision as to whether to introduce a record of achievement and the precise nature of the record were matters determined by the individual school. The raising of the school leaving age to 16 in the 1970s resulted in a plethora of diverse new schemes and initiatives being used in schools, all having one common feature, that of a school leaving certificate.[1]

At this time, the government, represented by the Department of Education and Science (DES), was playing no part, except in publishing accounts of the Schools Council on the development of records in some schools.

In 1983, the DES published a draft policy statement on Records of Achievement and announced its intention to carry out experimental work on the basis of which it would develop a National Record of Achievement for use in secondary schools in England and Wales. This was warmly welcomed by a wide range of interest groups, as was the 1984 DES Policy Statement, stating the intention of setting in place arrangements, by 1990, under which all young people would have records of achievement on leaving school.

Pilot schemes, DES-funded and evaluated by a Records of Achievement National Steering Committee (RANSC) yielded rich data and the final RANSC report was widely circulated with the expectation that RoAs would become mandatory in 1990.[2] However, in August 1990, the DES announced its decision that matters concerning RoAs should, after all, be decided by the schools.[3]

Definition

Despite the widespread interest in and support for matters concerning RoAs, there would appear to be little agreement on the precise meaning of the expression.

The Times Educational Supplement, which reports and comments on developments generally in education, first included the term 'Record of Achievement' in 1976.[4] Some writers use the term 'Profile' rather than 'Record of Achievement' but appear to attach the same meaning to it. In 1977, the first article concerned with RoAs appeared in the journal *Educational Research* and was entitled, 'Pupils in Profile'.[5] One writer, Law, defines profiling as 'a way of saying what is known about students'.[6] Law's book represents a range of profile formats but he points out that not all are called 'profiles' by their designers: some are called 'Student or Trainee Reviews', some 'Records of Experience' or 'Records of Achievement'. Research published by the Schools Council in 1982 has as its title *Profile reports for School Leavers*, yet in 1983 its follow-up publication was called *Recording Achievement at 16+*.

Practitioners in schools have now generally dropped the terms 'profile' or 'profiling' and talk about Records of Achievement and the processes of recording and reviewing. In HE, however, the term 'profiling' is currently being used to describe the same kinds of formative processes as those enjoyed by pupils in schools: processes of empowering students to be involved in the assessment, recording and reviewing of their own personal development and learning.[7] Central to any characterization of recording or reviewing would be dialogue between students and tutors, where students are encouraged to reflect on experience, to give and receive feedback, diagnose strengths and weaknesses and agree future learning targets and action plans.

The formative process is, then, at the heart of development, but many would see the production of an end document or summative record as equally important to students, employers and other 'end users' of such documents in that they provide a more rounded picture of an individual than a narrow list of examination results. A narrowly-defined RoA might describe only certain aspects of the process, rather than acknowledge that 'process' and 'product' dimensions operate simultaneously.

In this book, writers have themselves used a wide variety of terms and titles in connection with recording achievement. All have in common, however, the idea that profiling or recording achievement is a process which involves students in recording, reviewing and reflecting on their own experience, to turn it into learning which empowers them to become more confident, self aware and capable people.

The National Record of Achievement (NRA)

There is a great deal of interest in profiling and recording achievement in HE at the present time. One reason for this interest is the introduction of the National Record of Achievement (NRA). In March 1991, in a joint venture, the DES and the Employment Department issued some 20,000 free sample copies of an NRA to schools, colleges and employers, inviting them to use it as they saw fit, but making it clear that they were under no obligation to do so.

In December 1992, the Secretary of State for Education endorsed the NRA and issued Circular 14/92, rendering the record mandatory, with effect from January 1993. [8] In Summer 1993, all school leavers will be required by law to take with them an NRA which meets the new regulations. This will have profound implications for FE and HE institutions, not only in terms of their admissions policies, but for the way in which they deliver their courses, for teaching and learning styles and for assessment. Students will be bringing with them not only an RoA but a host of expectations. They will be expecting to be responsible for influencing the nature and content of their courses. They will expect flexibility and choice, freedom to negotiate, the right to be involved in the production of their references and records, and to assess their own and their peers' work. Through Education for Capability and Young Enterprise, students will want the opportunity to solve problems, make decisions and manage themselves, working in collaboration with peers on real and relevant problems and projects.

The NRA is also used by another player on the field: the National Council for Vocational Qualifications (NCVQ), formed in 1986. This organization kitemarks all vocational qualifications, which then take the form of elements and units of competence, recorded on the NRA. Increasing numbers of applicants to HE will be coming with NVQs, instead of O or A levels, and these will be documented on their NRA. NCVQ has recently developed GNVQs (General National Vocational Qualifications) which, unlike NVQs, are not specific to a particular vocational area. In 1989, the remit of NCVQ was extended to include professional and higher education and it is kitemarking degree level qualifications. It is likely, then, that the NRA will be used within HE.

Profiling and 'accessibility'

A second reason for the interest is that people of many political persuasions are advocating increased 'access' to HE. The White Paper, *Higher Education: a*

New Framework (1991) and the Further and Higher Education Act (1992)[9] commit the government to expanding participation rates in HE, but not just to providing 'more of the same'; rather, the White Paper sets out to facilitate the production of a body of graduates equipped to deal with the demands of a rapidly changing working environment. The Paper, like its predecessor, *Higher Education: Meeting The Challenge*,[10] aims to build on the broad education increasingly provided in schools.

Access in the traditional sense – the attempt to find ways of helping groups or individuals to enter HE – is giving way to 'accessibility': the attempt to change the organization and culture of HE. Access, traditionally, is concerned with maintaining demand for HE, and not in altering what is supplied.[11] The priority of 'accessibility', on the other hand, is to change HE to meet student needs.

A number of developments reflect the overall aim of increasing the accessibility of HE. Barbara Pearce, director of Leeds University Careers Counselling and Development Unit summarized some of them: 'Modularization, Credit Accumulation and Transfer (CATS), access for non-traditional students.'[12] Students can record the learning from each module – whether it be work-based learning, a unit of an English literature course, or the results of a computing programme – on their profiles/RoAs.

Skills capabilities

A third reason for the interest in profiling at the moment is the increasing focus, within HE, on skills and capabilities.

The RSA's Education for Capability programme stresses student-centred learning designed to facilitate the development of 'core' skills such as communication, problem-solving and group work. HEC says: 'Capability is best promoted and motivation enhanced if learners exercise responsibility, take initiatives, are creative and cooperate within their learning programmes'.[13] 'Capable' students possess excellence not just in acquiring knowledge, but in 'using and communicating knowledge, in doing, making, designing, collaborating and creating'.[14] RoAs 'have the potential for giving students real experience of being responsible and accountable for their own experience whilst on courses'.[15]

Since 1987, the Department of Employment's Enterprise in Higher Education (EHE) programme has been funding institutional projects with the overall aim of of developing the 'enterprise' skills of students. Instead of focusing exclusively on the knowledge gained in programmes of learning, academics and students are thinking increasingly about the transferable and 'transferring' skills students are acquiring whilst in HE.

Transferable skills include the cognitive qualities of abstraction and conceptualization as well as the better-known aptitudes of communication, literacy and numeracy. There is then a further set of skills which arise from the question: how do these kinds of skill acquired in one context 'transfer' to another? For example, how do communication skills gained in the context of a business studies course transfer to the work environment? These 'transferring' skills[16] are perhaps the most important, but the most elusive. Students need to gain some understanding of how 'transferable' skills are acquired; they will need 'a larger framework of understanding' or a model of how skills are transferred.[17] Profiling can help build up this model by encouraging reflection on the learning process and by facilitating an understanding of how assessments relate to learning objectives.

Several EHE institutions recognize the connection between the development of 'transferable' or 'core' skills and profiling. At North London University, for example, half of the funding available for EHE projects on skills development is being directed towards the development, by groups of staff, students and employers, of appropriate profiles for their subject area.[18]

Careers education and work-based learning

The focus on skills invites students to think about the sort of person they might be or might become; it is an aspect of careers education.[19] Profiling can be used by a student to focus in on particular career options, or it can be employed as a device, within the workplace, for thinking about professional development. As Bob Bellis put it:

. . . the firm introduced two years ago an enhanced careers development programme. It was designed to encourage staff, early on in their careers, to think about how they are developing professionally and personally, about the sorts of things they find most satisfying and what sort of work they might like to be doing in the future.[20]

A personal work book supported this plan.

Relatedly, there is the move towards accrediting work-based learning, reflected partly in the huge number of Employment Department-funded projects in this area. Occasionally, an individual can receive a whole degree qualification based on workplace experience. Large numbers, however, are receiving part of their award through accredited experience. There is the move to accredit prior learning (APL) or assess prior experience (APEL). The results of any or all of these processes can be documented on an RoA.

The following chapters expand on or develop some of the themes outlined here.

References

1. Schools Council (1965) *Working Paper No. 2, Raising the School Leaving Age, a Cooperative Programme for Research and Development*, HMSO, London.
2. Department of Education and Science and the Welsh Office (1989) *Records of Achievement. Report of the Records of Achievement National Steering Committee*, DES, London.
3. Department of Education and Science (1990) *The Education (Individual Pupils' Achievements) (Information) Regulations 1990*, Circular 8/90, DES, London.

4. *The Times Educational Supplement* (Scotland), August 1976.
5. Wilson, E (1977) 'Pupils in profile: Making the most of teachers' knowledge of pupils', *Educational Research*, 20.
6. Law, B (1984) *Uses and Abuses of Profiling: A handbook of reviewing and recording students' experience and achievement*, Harper and Row, London.
7. See, for example, Fenwick A, Assiter A and Nixon N (1992) *Profiling in HE*, CNAA, London.
8. This information derives from the Annual Reports and the EHE Newsletter of the various institutions.
9. DES (1991) *Higher Education: A new framework*, White Paper CM1541, London, HMSO.
10. DES (1992) *Higher Education: Meeting the challenge*, White Paper CM 9254, London, HMSO.
11. See, for example, Peter Wright (1991) 'Access or accessibility', *Journal of Access Studies*, 6, 1, Spring.
12. These remarks were made at the opening of the 'Using RoAs in HE' conference in 1992 in Wakefield.
13. These remarks were made by John Stephenson at the opening of the 'Using RoAs in HE' conference in 1992 in Wakefield.
14. Stephenson, J and Weil, S (1991) *Higher Education for Capability*, *Summary Report*.
15. John Stephenson in his introductory remarks to the conference, 'Using Records of Achievement in Higher Education, Leeds, 1992.
16. Bridges, D (1992) 'Transferable Skills: A philosophical perspective', *Studies in Higher Education*, Summer.
17. Taylor, D (1993) 'Dancing about in architecture', *EHE News*, North London University, Spring.
18. North London University (1992) *Annual EHE Report*.
19. Watt, T and Hawthorn, R (1992) NICEC Report, 'Careers education and the curriculum in HE', CRAC, Cambridge.
20. Rob Bellis, in his introductory remarks to the 'Using RoAs in HE' conference in 1992 in Wakefield.

Chapter Two

Profiling in Higher Education
Alison Assiter and Angela Fenwick

Between August 1990 and July 1992, the CNAA undertook two projects on profiling in HE: Profiling Work-based Learning in Academic Courses, funded by the Employment Department, and Recording Student Achievements in CNAA Courses, funded by the CNAA. The projects set out to produce guidelines on introducing and using profiling systems both for programmes of learning based in CNAA institutions and for work-based learning at HE level.

This chapter outlines the methodology employed by the project teams, illustrates the different types of profiling system revealed by the research and sets out some key points for discussion.

Methodology for profiling projects

At the outset of both projects, all CNAA course leaders (approximately 2,500) were sent a letter asking whether they had used any kind of profiling system either for assessing students' work-based learning or for the assessment of learning within other components of the course. The response was encouraging; in all, 250 courses claimed to be using a profiling system of some kind. The majority of responses were from the subject areas of teacher training, management studies, professions allied to medicine and the creative arts. By contrast, very few responses were received from the disciplines of humanities, social science, engineering and the pure sciences.

A sample of 24 profiling systems was selected from which fairly detailed case studies were carried out. The sample was deliberately targeted so that the whole subject range was represented, even though the response to the letter had been very low in some subject areas. The case studies involved interviews with a selection of relevant academic staff, work-based 'mentors' and students, using a framework questionnaire. Guidelines on how to develop and use a profiling system were then written using information gleaned from each of the case studies. The profiling work-based learning project then commissioned 12 course leaders to carry out feasibility studies of the guidelines as well as to participate in a number of subject-area working groups.

Main types of profiling systems identified

The projects identified the following three types of profile. They are inter-linked and may be used in conjunction with each other; the way they are all used will depend on the purposes and functions of each.

The prescribed learning outcomes profile

Within this type of profile the outcomes of learning from a component of a programme or the course as a whole, are identified and described. These prescribed learning outcomes form the framework for the teaching, learning and assessment processes and provide students with clearly defined goals against which to target learning. Such a system may be useful for professionally orientated courses which require learners to achieve a set of objectives in order to obtain a licence to practise or enter a profession.

The negotiated learning outcomes profile

This type of profile is different from the above in that learners play a much greater part in characterizing their own learning outcomes. It may be particularly appropriate for components of courses where learners have differing experiences and therefore varied achievements.

In addition to identifying and describing their own learning outcomes, students can negotiate:

- the way in which the learning outcomes can be achieved, ie, the tasks that need to be carried out and the skills that need to be developed;
- the way in which the achievement or development of the learning outcome will be measured;
- what evidence is required in order to prove that the learning outcome has been achieved.

The personal development profile

This profile is used for the formative assessment of students' learning and/or personal development and is usually conducted through self-assessment. Learners plot their own development against a set of objectives or intended learning outcomes. Personal development profiles are often similar to the diaries, journals and logbooks with which many courses are familiar, especially within work-based components of programmes of learning. This type appeared to be taken more seriously by all parties if it was integrated into the course in some way: for example, if it was used to provide a framework for tutorials or was used in conjunction with the other types of profile mentioned above and linked to the programme of study.

A summary of the main issues arising from the research

A key point to emerge from the research is that the documentation itself is less significant than the processes which underpin its production; the documentation serves to support these processes. Profiling invites a focus on the learner as opposed to the course or the subject, encouraging a more learner-centred approach to learning and teaching. Learning may take place in a variety of contexts: for example, the home, the workplace or the educational establishment, and learning gained in any of these contexts can be recorded on a profile. For most traditional courses, then, profiling involves thinking about the intended outcomes of learning: what a person will have achieved either from a programme of study or from a particular type of experience.

The following issues represent some of the key 'guidance' points (they summarize the key points in the document *Profiling in HE*)[1] that may be of value to anyone developing a profiling system:

1. All the systems which were studied were being continually developed and refined. Emphasis should therefore be given to the *developmental nature* of the process of introducing and using profiling systems of whatever type.

2. Thought should be given, prior to the development of any system, to what the *purpose(s)* of the system will be. For example:
   - Is it to provide a record of learners' achievements in a particular component of a programme (eg, a work placement)? If so, what will the record be used for?
   - Is it to provide a framework for self-assessment? If so, will the results of the assessment be used:
     — for learners' own use to provide a record of their personal development and/or
     — to provide evidence of the achievement of the learning objectives which are integral to the programme?

3. All parties who will use the profiling system in some way should have an *input* into its initial development.

4. *Learning outcomes, assessment criteria and evidence* need to be identified and described. How and in what detail will depend on the nature of the profiling system.

5. *Quantifying/grading* the achievement of learning outcomes is an issue. Is it necessary to incorporate a grading scale? If so, careful attention will need to be paid to its wording and construction.

6. Procedures for ensuring *formative assessment* are vital (except in the case of some types of accreditation of prior learning).

7. Profiling should not simply be an add-on to existing processes, rather it should be *fully integrated* into teaching and learning processes and curriculum development.

8. *Training and staff development* is required for:
   - learners
   - academic staff
   - workplace assessors
   - mentors
   - external examiners

9. *Equal opportunity issues* should be considered. For example:
   - Does the wording of any profile components discriminate between women/men; different ethnic groups; those from different class backgrounds?
   - Is the image of the 'competent practitioner' biased in any of the above ways? For example, were the learning outcomers formulated from an image of a white, middle-class, male practitioner?
   - Does the process favour one group, eg, mature learners against 18-year-olds?
   - Are any of the supporting mechanisms discriminatory? For example, is there a heavy reliance on self-assessment tools which may benefit a more 'confident' group at the expense of people who may be less self-assured?
   - Are there procedures in place so that anybody who feels that they have been discriminated against can appeal? (The appeals procedure should not replicate the problem).
   - Are learners being asked to provide evidence which does not, in fact, relate to any of the required learning outcomes and which may, in consequence, discriminate against them actually achieving or developing the necessary learning outcomes?

10. Profiling systems should be evaluated to ensure their effectiveness. *Quality assurance* procedures, both internal and external, should be developed and monitored.

11. *Resourcing* the introduction and use of a profiling system needs careful consideration. The initial 'cost' of development may be offset by the long-term benefits. For example:
    - Profiling provides a means whereby the student can make an easier (and therefore, less dependent on staff) transition from one course or work setting to another.
    - It can save time at the interfaces between parts of courses, or courses and the outside world, by documenting the knowledge and skills which a learner already possesses.
    - Within courses, both the 'course' and any 'workplace' assessment can be more usefully integrated by providing a common framework.
    - Any apparent separateness between different settings/contexts can begin to be broken down, thus facilitating more APL to take place.

Reference

1. CNAA (1992) *Profiling in HE*, CNAA, London.

Part Two:

The Experience

SECTION 1:
USING RECORDS OF ACHIEVEMENT AND PORTFOLIOS FOR ACCESS, ADMISSIONS AND ACCREDITATION OF PRIOR LEARNING

Introduction

Records of Achievement are invaluable tools when it comes to accrediting prior experience, whether it be conventional school experience, work-based learning or other types of learning or experience. School leavers, increasingly, are coming to higher education with a RoA (see Chapter 1) which might complement or eventually reduce present-day reliance on A-level scores as the primary evidence on which to base decisions on entry into higher education. The National Record of Achievement (NRA) contains sections which can record the results of examinations, but it also includes a section where individuals can offer a personal statement about their skills, qualities and achievements. The standardized format of the NRA as outlined in FE Circular 14/92 ('Reports on individual pupils' achievement', DfE, 1992) provides scope for a fairer and more rational admissions procedure into HE. A major project, located in Wigan, with Rob Ward as the project manager, is looking at improving awareness of the scope of RoAs in the admissions procedures into HE.

The chapters by Richard Gretton and Heather Hughes Jones describe some work that is being conducted in the use of RoDs in the admissions process to HE. Gretton's article describes the result of a research project involving the University of Brighton, Roehampton Institute and the University of Sussex and a debate on the incorporation of information about a student's RoA onto the University Central Council on Admissions (UCCA)/Polytechnics Central Admissions System (PCAS) forms.

Hughes Jones outlines the operation of the Bolton Institute Passport scheme, which provides a route into HE for people with potential but who are underachieving. In the scheme, Bolton Institute works in partnership with two sixth form colleges and their feeder schools.

Profiling additionally provides an invaluable means of documenting the results of prior experience or prior learning, as the chapter by Nyatanga and Fox demonstrates. The results of one's prior experience or prior learning can be documented on a profile and, once there are standardized types of documentation for this, a credible means of recognizing prior achievement would become available. Of course, the steps in this direction are difficult ones: agreeing the format for such documentation is a formidable task. But increasing numbers of people are agreed on the value of recognizing and accrediting prior experience and prior learning. Accreditation of Prior Learning (APL) or Assessment of Prior Experiential Learning (APEL) increases access and equal opportunities by documenting skills and achievements which would otherwise go unrecognized and unrecorded.

Howard Foster's chapter examines ways in which the portfolio can be used in National Vocational Qualifications (NVQs) and its role not only in preparing students for employment, but as a tool for self-development.

Chapter Three

Records of Achievement and Admissions to Higher Education

Richard Gretton

The context

Records of Achievement developments within schools and colleges which were undertaken after the publication in 1984 of the DES policy statement focused initially for the most part on the 11–16 age group.[1] As the benefits of both the formative *process* and the summative *product* became increasingly apparent, it was logical for the work to continue with other age groups: hence the subsequent work with post-16 and primary students.

The pilot work that was being developed across the country was monitored by the Records of Achievement National Steering Committee (RANSC). Its report of 1989 identified two key issues:

- 'The provision of a more comprehensive record (of achievement) should . . . be of benefit to . . . further and higher education tutors in selection for and in pursuit of training or further courses of study.'
- 'Further and higher education institutions . . . should build on the record of achievement, ensuring a sound basis for the continued recording of new achievements and experiences and the further development of skills.'[2]

At the same time, many changes were being experienced in HE. Work supported by the then Training Agency had reflected in particular on the situation being faced by HE in relation to admissions issues:

- 'British higher education is at a turning point at the present time. It is clear that much of the growth in student numbers which has taken place in recent years has not been accompanied by changes in admission mechanisms – indeed, the recent unforeseen buoyancy in demand has convinced many institutions that no major changes are necessary.'

- 'However, change will undoubtedly be needed if we are to turn away from a highly selective system towards one which, by accommodating and welcoming participants of all ages, from all social groups . . . and with a wide range of previous experience, deserves the title of "mass higher education". We believe that HE on a mass scale is required, not to meet the survival needs of institutions and departments, but to meet the need for a more highly educated labour force and from a sense of justice to all groups in society . . .'

- '. . . We believe that in institutions and departments the basic criterion for admissions should be a candidate's ability to complete his or her chosen course. Policies that give automatic priority to high A-Level applicants should be regarded as educationally unsound and inappropriate, because they disregard the potential of "non-standard" and lower A Level applicants . . .'.[3]

Alongside these developments, debate has continued on the appropriateness of the current post-16 curriculum as a preparation for HE:

- 'University Vice-Chancellors are again questioning the value of A-levels as passports to a campus education.'

- '(The Secretary of State at the DES) . . . is struggling to find a way of broadening sixth form education and mixing vocational and academic subjects, yet maintaining A-levels as some sort of gold standard.'

- 'Vice-Chancellors supported a package of proposals to widen access in a way that could finally put paid to their campuses as three-year homes for middle class young adults'.[4]

Equally, the mission statement of Higher Education for Capability (HEC) is congruent with this context:

'Individuals, industry and society will all benefit from a well balanced education concerned not only with academic excellence in the acquisition of knowledge and skills of analysis but also with excellence in using and communicating knowledge, doing, making, designing, collaborating and creating.'[5]

For many involved in RoA developments, it was recognized that here was an opportunity to use RoAs creatively to support work both in post-16 and HE and as part of the admissions mechanism.

Admissions to Higher Education project

This led to the setting up of a pilot with funding from the Employment Department Group to explore these issues in greater detail. The project has involved three HE institutions (Brighton Polytechnic, Roehampton Institute and the University of Sussex) and six LEAs (Bexley, Hampshire, Kingston, Merton, Surrey and Sutton).

Work has been undertaken with staff and students in post-16 schools and colleges to support the development of formative systems of recording achievement. This has encouraged greater use of tutorial support in reviewing the students' progress and has led to more systematic recording of achievements and experiences, particularly in relation to short- and medium-term targets. This work has been significantly aided by the parallel development in many post-16 institutions of systems of Individual Action Planning.

Timing: interim and final RoAs

Schools and colleges originally were working towards the production of a final summative document around Easter of Year 13 (upper sixth). However, it was recognized that this could only make a marginal contribution to the admissions to HE cycle, as it is currently organized.

Pilot schools and colleges have therefore changed many of their reporting arrangements and now look to the production of an interim RoA at the end of Year 12 (lower sixth). This has had a number of benefits:

- the students have had an opportunity to reflect at length on their most recent academic and personal achievements, particularly in relation to their skills and qualities;
- this has helped to set the context of their thinking over the summer in relation to:
  - whether they wish to apply to HE
  - which courses interest them
  - to which HE institutions they wish to apply;
- it has provided an invaluable source document for them to begin drafting the further information section on the UCCA/PCAS application form at the beginning of Year 13;
- it has enabled them to attempt to match their own achievements, experiences, skills and qualities to those that are required for the courses they have in mind (where information about the selection criteria has been available).
- if invited for interview, it has been valuable in supporting the applicants' preparation and, from the increased experience of one-to-one interviews in school/college, the students have developed greater confidence in talking about their achievements, experiences, strengths *and* weaknesses;
- it has provided the students with an opportunity to put together a portfolio of supporting evidence to which reference could be made at interview: this might include examples of coursework, accredited information on work-related experience and extra-curricular activities which are linked to the course for which the student has applied;
- as a source document for the school/college to compile the referee's statement: some schools already use verbatim extracts from a student's interim or final RoA in place of a confidential reference, stating this on the application form.

Many schools and colleges then provide further opportunities for students to update their portfolios and summative statements during Year 13, producing a final summary document for presentation shortly before the end of the year. This would then be available for students to forward to HE institutions from which they had received offers to be available as supplementary information at confirmation, after examination results are published. Following confirmation, the RoA could also provide information which could be used to support and enhance induction programmes at the beginning of the HE course.

The UCCA/PCAS application form

Changes in the structure of the UCCA/PCAS application form over the past two years have been helpful. The form used by applicants for 1991 entry had eight lines of space to provide their further information. On the 1992 entry form, two significant changes were made: the space available increased to 26 lines; and a question asking, 'Does the applicant have a Record of Achievement?' was included in the administrative questions answered by the applicant's post-16 institution on page 4 of the application form.

Research into a randomly selected sample of application forms (for 1992 entry) received at Brighton Polytechnic, Roehampton Institute and the University of Sussex revealed the following information in response to the Record of Achievement question:

	Female	Male	Totals	%
Yes	54	37	91	15.9
No entry	57	45	102	17.8
No	219	162	381	66.4
Totals	330	244	574	

There were no significant differences between the genders:

	Female %	Male %
Yes	16.4	15.2
No entry	17.3	18.4
No	66.4	66.4

What was most disturbing about these findings was the relatively high proportion of applications on which no information about the students' RoA was provided. This prompted a debate with UCCA and PCAS which proposed the following:

- the relocation of the question in the section completed by the applicant;
- this would reflect a crucial aspect of RoA development work which is the student's *ownership* of the process and product;
- a change of wording to, 'Do you have a post-16 Record of Achievement?' to recognize that some students' schools/colleges had previously

answered, 'Yes', when in fact the RoA referred to had been completed much earlier in Year 11 (fifth year) and had not been subsequently updated;

● the removal of the pre-printed hatched lines to enable applicants to print out an extract from their RoA and for it to be legible.

The proposals supported suggestions made elsewhere and all these changes were made to the UCCA/PCAS form recently published for 1993 entry. The question now reads, 'Do you have an up-to-date (post-16) Record of Achievement?'; the lines in Section 9 are printed in yellow, as a guide to those handwriting the section, but do not appear when photocopied; the number of lines available has increased from 26 to 32.

In my experience, schools and colleges have unanimously welcomed the changes to the UCCA/PCAS application form of the past two years. They feel that their students now have a much better opportunity to provide information which can be considered by admissions tutors and that the quality of the students' data has significantly improved. Certainly the quantity of it has increased: the sample of 1992 entry forms revealed that the increased space was being used.

No. of lines used in Section 9A	No. of Applicants	% of sample
13 or more	574	100.0
20 or more	530	92.3
23 or more	490	85.4
Either 25 or all 26	424	73.9

Research with admissions tutors in 16 schools of study/departments across the three participating HE institutions in relation to the 1991/2 admissions exercise has revealed some interesting information. Asked whether the expansion in space in Section 9A had been useful, 62.5 per cent said 'Yes', 37.5 per cent said 'No'. Has the quality of information improved? – 'Yes', 50 per cent; 'no perceptible difference', 50 per cent.

Only half of the respondents said that they actually read all of the information in Section 9A. This clearly is a reflection in many of the departments concerned of the sheer dimensions of the task involved. There was some significant concern expressed that some of the student data were extremely difficult to read this year: the process of photo-reduction that each form went through this year at Cheltenham before forwarding to the HE institutions clearly did not go entirely smoothly. This is obviously com-pounded on some occasions by the quality of the applicant's handwriting.

The use of the RoA at the time of interview

In the schools of study/departments within the sample, relatively few students actually had an RoA. Some of the findings are necessarily thin on research evidence. However, these comments may be helpful:

- none of the departments had asked students to send extracts in advance of interview, but 25 per cent had asked them to bring their RoA with them to interview, if they had one;
- 31 per cent indicated that they would have preferred to have had sight of the RoA before the interview;
- four departments asked for photocopies of appropriate extracts to be left behind after interview and these were taken into account when decisions about offers were being made;
- evidence in the RoA was felt to be useful and was sufficiently up-to-date;
- where appropriate, some admissions tutors initiated discussion about the applicant's RoA; in 25 per cent of cases, the student had initiated discussion about the RoA;
- there was evidence from interviewers that the performance of interviewees who had an RoA had been affected for the better; students demonstrated greater confidence to discuss their achievements and experiences and the evidence behind their motivation and commitment towards the particular course of study for which they had applied;
- students appeared to be sufficiently skilled in using the RoA: this clearly reflected the preparation by the students and their tutors, for example in mock/practice interviews.

This final aspect must not be taken for granted though: generally, research has revealed that although schools developing RoAs have recognized the formative benefits of developing the process and the documentation, they have given insufficient emphasis to preparing students in how they use the summary document.

Expanding the use of RoAs

At this stage of the development, some admissions tutors remain cautious about whether they would wish to see all applicants having an RoA to support their application. Indeed, tutors in many schools and colleges are concerned to see evidence from HE of appropriate interest in RoAs before committing the necessary time and resources to their continued development.

There is no linear progression to this initiative: it is very much a cyclical/spiral development route. Indeed, it is very much a question of the chicken and the egg: schools/colleges would develop RoAs if HE was demonstrating genuine interest; HE would be taking them more seriously if the frequency with which they were presented with RoAs was increasing significantly. We are very much at an early stage but the likelihood is that, with the NRA now available, an ever-increasing number of post-16 RoAs will be produced.

Confidentiality

One part of recent research has related to confidentiality. RoAs are generally held to be the outcome of an openly discussed and negotiated dialogue between students and tutors. For many schools and colleges, a confidential reference is incompatible with this approach. The instructions from UCCA/ PCAS for 1993 entry have reiterated that all references are treated as confidential. However, they have acknowledged that '. . . some schools and colleges operate a system whereby references are discussed between the applicant and the teaching staff possibly as part of the process of reviewing and recording achievement'. Referees are then advised that they '. . . may wish to indicate . . . whether or not the admissions tutors may openly discuss the reference with the applicant'

The research into 1992 entry revealed that very few references currently give any indication that they have either been seen by the applicant or that he or she has made any contribution to it. Just over 1 per cent of the sample of application forms that were reviewed had a sentence indicating that they were verbatim extracts from an RoA; amongst those, just over 4 per cent gave an indication of the student's involvement in its drafting.

Asked whether references should be completely closed, 56 per cent of the departments questioned felt they should. Only one respondent felt they should be completely open but the remainder considered that they could be mostly open with a small proportion of the reference remaining confidential. This might include background information about either the applicant's home or school circumstances, for example. Interestingly, over 90 per cent of students interviewed on this matter considered that it was in order for their school/college to reserve the right to state something confidential about them. The vast majority of students welcomed the chance to know most of what was being written about them, particularly as it was often more positive than they had anticipated.

There was one area that needed further development work. Admissions tutors were asked what their personal reactions would be to a reference which they knew to be 'open' in some way: 13.3 per cent indicated that their reaction would be enhanced and that they would have greater confidence in the information in the reference; 40 per cent indicated no difference in their reaction. However, 46.7 per cent indicated that their reaction might in some way be damaged and that they might have less confidence in the reference.

This finding cannot be directly extrapolated to work on RoAs. However, I believe this does reflect a significant need for staff development in reflecting on the relative merits of information drafted with the applicant's involvement.

Conclusion

I believe there is evidence of a willingness within HE to consider the structural and curricular implications of moving towards an admissions mechanism based much more on descriptive information rather than grades. Moves towards greater modularization, wider availability of credit accumulation and transfer schemes, semesterization and improvements in guidance and counselling arrangements are all congruent with the development of RoAs.

There are many parallels with work in secondary schools in the mid-1980s and concerns about time, resources and the threat to the status quo are continuing. However, it is of paramount importance that we do not lose sight of the immense potential benefits of the *process* of RoAs. By giving students greater responsibility for their own learning and assessment, we can provide a springboard for significant improvements in motivation, commitment and standards of performance.

References

1.   DES/Welsh Office (1984) Policy Statement, HMSO.

2.   DES/Welsh Office (1989) *Records of Achievement*. Report of the Records of Achievement National Steering Committee, DES, London.

3.   Fulton, O and Ellwood, S (1989) *Admissions to Higher Education: Policy and Practice*, TA, Sheffield.

4.   The *Guardian*, October 1990.

5.   HEC (1992) Conference Papers, HEC, Wakefield.

Chapter Four

Passport Scheme
Heather Hughes Jones

Introduction

The Bolton Institute Passport scheme provides an example of the use of Records of Achievement in the transition to higher education. In this pilot scheme, Bolton Institute is in partnership with two sixth form colleges and their feeder schools to provide a route into HE for students with potential, but who, for recognized reasons, are underachieving. The details of the scheme are being determined in consultation with local schools, colleges and the Careers Service. As a result of these discussions, productive links with Bolton COMPACT have been developed.

The scheme provides attractions and benefits to the applicants, their schools and colleges and to the Institute. The applicants gain improved access to HE, helped by earlier contact, continuity of contact and improved knowledge of HE. The scheme provides for the possible mitigation of the negative effect of disadvantage on the application process. The schools and colleges should benefit from the improved admissions and subject links with the Institute. There should also be a beneficial impact on the staying-on rate and increased numbers proceeding to HE.

The scheme will help to meet the Institute's mission to provide wider access to HE. Participation in the scheme is demonstrating that our commitment to widening access extends beyond the more usual access practices, eg, recruiting mature access, to some of the educationally disadvantaged groups which are more difficult to reach. If the scheme leads

I should like to acknowledge the encouragement and advice received from Chris Topley who was responsible for the Passport scheme at Oxford Polytechnic. I should also like to acknowledge the input of colleagues involved in the Bolton Institute Passport scheme.

to increased numbers of *local* students enrolling, this may reduce pressure on accommodation. The scheme is enhancing links with local A-level providers at a number of levels (head teachers, careers and subject teachers, pupils and parents) thereby creating the basis for good long-term relationships.

Once beyond the pilot phase the Institute will need to formulate practical and justifiable limits for effective functioning of the scheme. Current thinking is to adopt an overall Institute limit of 5 per cent of intake with a 10 per cent upper limit on any one course and within that a flexible ceiling would need to be agreed with course teams. Full-time and sandwich courses at HND/degree level are included with no restriction on courses available. This is essential if the potential applicants are to have genuine access.

Operation of the pilot scheme

The scheme will involve identification of potential Passport students in Year 11 by the school or college COMPACT coordinators, together with other school staff. Typically the latter will include the year tutor or tutor with pastoral responsibility. It will also be important to include the LA careers officer who may be able to provide a wider base of information relevant to the process. Once the potential Passport scheme pupils have been identified, the Careers Service has indicated that this group could have early careers interviews. The Careers Service would have information on the pupil's academic ability, health, career ideas and spare time interests: possibly the careers officer could identify disadvantages affecting an individual pupil. Draft guidelines for identifying potential Passport applicants have been produced through consultation and discussion with partners (see the Appendix to this chapter).

The application is in two stages in Years 11 and 12. In Year 11 it is too early for a pupil to select and apply for an HE course so the aim is to identify potential Passport students, in terms of the guidelines in the Appendix. During Year 12 the second stage of the application takes place where students apply for specific courses. The Institute will provide, in collaboration with the schools, a programme for students involved with Passport at Years 11, 12 and 13 (which could be built into the COMPACT review system) of, for example, HE counselling, open days, special visits, taster courses, shadowing of existing students and schedules of guided reading.

An important aim is to provide regular links from the stage where the potential Passport students are identified through to the time the offer is made and until the place is taken up. Once enrolled the student will continue to receive support within the Institute.

Nature of offer

The offer must include some level of academic achievement through exam results, but should also lay stress on levels of motivation, attitudes, attendance, punctuality and skills and aptitudes as revealed by RoAs. These latter qualities (some judged subjectively) partially replace the 'normal' academic requirements. There will be opportunities for fruitful contact between the Passport scheme and the major project on RoAs based in Wigan in which the Institute is one of the HE partners.

In the pilot we shall be exploring how to incorporate Passport goals into the pupils' normal goal-setting and review system under the COMPACT scheme in Year 12.

An offer would be negotiated on an individual basis, but the grade component would be below the normal Institute level for that course. Negotiation could take place between the admissions tutor, applicant and the A-level provider. The pilot phase will address this issue and provide guidelines for practice. The offer would normally be made in Year 12, ie, before the student completes the PCAS/UCCA forms in Year 13. The offer is essentially a contract; once agreed the Institute is committed to honouring the offer if conditions are met. However, the student is not obliged to take a place after completing the terms of the Passport offer, but may choose to go elsewhere for higher education.

Issues which the Passport scheme has had to address

To be adopted, a Passport scheme must have the support of admissions tutors, schools and colleges as well as principals and head teachers. The Bolton Institute Passport scheme is being worked out initially through dialogue and, later, through practice in the pilot phase. The original outline was informed by principles established elsewhere but it has developed its own character through local circumstances. During this process a number of issues and questions have arisen. Some of these are described below and it is hoped that our experiences will provide some generalizable insights.

HEI concerns

- Will the overload on administration outweigh any benefits?
- Some staff think we have existing mechanism for recruiting this type of student.
- Will it lower standards?
- Some courses are subject to professional body validation and claim input standards cannot be varied.

These are real concerns but the answers cannot be provided in advance of the scheme's operation. It will take time and experience to gain confidence with alternatives to examination grade requirements. To put the concerns in context it should be said that they are outweighed by positive attitudes and that in the pilot the concerns will be addressed where possible.

Schools/sixth form colleges concerns

Although the pilot phase is limited to four schools and colleges, consultation and development has been wide. There has also been helpful input from the

FE college through the COMPACT coordinator. It was only through the discussion groups and meetings that these issues emerged. The need for a Passport scheme to be worked up collaboratively to meet local needs is probably the most important lesson. Some reactions include the following:

- *There are already too many new initiatives.*
  This first reaction to the proposed scheme should not be surprising given the following initiatives: the National Curriculum; TVEI; COMPACT; RoA, etc. However, progress became possible when it was realized that the Passport could link in to the existing framework for COMPACT.
- *Schools want a relationship with the Institute before committing themselves to the scheme.*
  We agree that it is important to build up links, mutual knowledge and trust before embarking on a complex new scheme. We have increased our local school link activities. Schemes therefore cannot be rushed.
- *How would the scheme fit with the role of the LA careers adviser/officer in the school/college?*
  The careers officer may have information relevant to the identification of the Passport applicants, eg, health factors.
- *Year 11 is too early for students to make HE choices.*
  This issue arose from an early version of the scheme where we realized we had to reach back to Year 11. However, Year 11 was seen to be too early for a full blown Passport application. With the help of the careers service input and teachers, the scheme was modified to include a Year 11 stage where potential Passport students could be identified for participation in the contact activities. Applications could then take place in Year 12, based on knowledge gained from the contact programme.
- *There is a need to link between schools and between years within schools.*
  The longitudinal nature of the scheme means there needs to be a link between the schools taking pupils to Year 11 and the sixth form colleges taking them for Years 12 and 13. Similarly, it is necessary to ensure links between years within a school. Fortunately the COMPACT scheme has an established structure in the pilot schools and colleges. Through meetings and staff development we are building into this structure.
- *There is a need for guidelines for identification of potential Passport applicants.*
  Originally the guidelines included examples under the heading of school/educational disadvantages which could be taken as criticisms of the school or college, eg, known lack of specialist teaching in physics, languages, etc. or known background of 'industrial unrest' or high turnover of teachers in Years 10 and 11. These were later modified. Head teachers were, not surprisingly, unhappy with the thought of their schools being described in those terms. However, as unwritten guidelines, these and other educational factors were said to be relevant considerations.
- *Is the scheme an A-level safety net?*
  A common misconception of the scheme is to regard it as an A-level

safety net for surprise failures. By the very nature of the scheme such individuals are not included and they should seek entry by other routes at clearing. Passport will rely on early identification, setting goals for admission, monitoring and support.

- *Economic hardship would still be a barrier to access.*
  Some teachers felt that Passport would be limited if no economic help was available to students in hardship. In the short term we have no additional help beyond the usual student hardship provision, but we will explore the possibility of bursaries and sponsorship.

Joint concerns

- *How to set new kinds of entry requirements?*
  This will require learning on both sides and it is hoped that the pilot phase will provide the basis. Goal setting, using RoA and building into the COMPACT structure are just some of the issues ahead.
- *Creating longer-term progression/career plans for pupils and students.*
  Working on longer-term career plans will, to some extent, be a new experience for staff. Institute admissions staff who are accustomed to fairly restricted admissions contact (PCAS form, perhaps interview or open days) will be developing contact programmes with individual Passport applicants lasting for more than one year.
- *Need to allow time to build up relationships.*
  So far in the Bolton scheme there has been a rippling out effect where the number of relevant parties (outside the Institute) gradually increased as the scheme has developed. The scheme started with contacts in the LEA, then secondary heads, then Year tutors. Contact widened to include Bolton COMPACT, the COMPACT coordinators and the Careers Service. As the pilot progresses, other groups will become involved, eg, governors, pupils and families.

The 'Scheme Diary' below gives an indication of the timescale for the Bolton scheme.

SCHEME DIARY

1991 Summer   Visit to Oxford Polytechnic to learn about their scheme.

1991 Autumn term Draft paper leading to academic board presentation and endorsement.

1992 Spring term Meetings with Institute admissions tutors to explain/ discuss scheme.
Discussions with LEA officers.
Presentation to Bolton secondary heads group (team led by principal).
First meeting of Bolton secondary schools and Institute staff at the Institute (presentation, informal discussion groups, working party set up).

                            Passport incorporated into the mission statement as
                            part of the Institute's access mission.

1992 Summer term   Working party set up, several meetings and report
                            produced with recommendations.
                            Meeting with Bolton COMPACT (Education
                            Partnership) to present scheme.
                            Second meeting of secondary schools and Institute
                            staff to receive report – decision to pilot the scheme.
                            First meeting of COMPACT co-ordinators from
                            secondary schools and colleges (four) in the pilot
                            scheme to discuss staff development needs.

1992 Summer   Further discussion with careers service. Draft of two-
                            stage application forms.

Appendix: Guidelines for identifying potential Passport participants

The scheme provides an access route into HE at Bolton Institute for recognized underachievers. These are pupils with ability but who, for one reason or another, are not working to their full potential, but who would benefit from participation in this scheme. In the attempt to quantify what is meant by 'ability' it is proposed to take as a starting point the minimum entry qualifications normally requested by Bolton sixth form colleges, which is four GCSEs at grade C or above. Passport students may have had their performance affected by one or more of the following:

1. *Social disadvantage* –
    pupils with limited aspirations due to lack of awareness of the value of higher education and the opportunities available;
    little or no family experience of full-time education beyond statutory schooling;
    special responsibility for siblings or other family members (especially in one-parent families);
    working long hours in a job or other commitment outside school/ college.
2. *Ethnic minority*, eg, language/cultural barriers to HE, particularly into non-traditional areas.
3. *Special educational factor*
4. *Gender* in relation to the proposed course, eg, girls and science.
5. *Health* or other relevant factors identified by the careers officer.

Chapter Five

Recording of Achievement within Accreditation of Prior Learning: A Case for Three Capabilities

Lovemore Nyatanga and Jane Fox

Introduction

This chapter has been influenced mainly by research into good practice in the accreditation of prior learning (APL).[1] Across many institutions[2] there is an increased recognition that significant learning occurs within as well as outside formal settings. There is also further recognition that APL portfolio construction and subsequent assessment now forms the vital link between the individual's experience and creditable learning. Thus, amongst the many issues uncovered through the research into good practice in APL, this chapter will focus on the capability triangle as the most important factor in the recording of achievement within a portfolio. This triangle is made up of:

- student capability to make the claim and to provide relevant evidence;
- staff capability, in particular that of admission tutors, to assess and recommend credits for the learning provided and proved through APL portfolio;
- organizational capability to recognize the centrality of APL not only to access/admission to higher education but also to equal opportunity.

Before focusing on the capability triangle and its relevance for APL portfolio construction and assessment, a functional definition of APL needs to be articulated.

Definition of APL

APL is a process that enables people of all ages, backgrounds and social standing to receive credit for learning they have acquired. According to the Open University,[3] the basic premise of APL is that people can and indeed do learn throughout their lives in a variety of settings. Traditionally, there has been an attempt to distinguish the accreditation of prior learning (APL) from the accreditation of prior experiential learning (APEL). The essence of the distinction revolves around the actual sources of capability or learning. For instance, APL assumes that the learning to be credited has come from formal activities such as conferences, workshops, short courses and so on while APEL assumes that the learning or capability to be credited has come from informal activities (more general life experiences) such as bringing up a family, pursuing a hobby, travel, and so on. From this distinction it can be seen that APEL is intended to attract the non-traditional entrant to HE through systematic recognition of prior learning and giving credit where credit is due.[4]

Recording of APL capability

Current research has shown that even the most capable of students do not ordinarily possess skills necessary for the reflectivity and subsequent articulation of their prior learning. These necessary skills may be summarised with the acronym SISE:[5]

S = systematic reflection on prior experience

I = identification of significant learning or capabilities

S = synthesis of relevant evidence through APL portfolio

E = evaluation of evidence by admission tutors or APL team.

The research carried out between November 1990 and June 1992 has also shown that good practice in APL requires that:

- clear guidance be given on portfolio construction;
- the criteria for portfolio assessment or any other approaches including all rules of the engagement are publicly declared in advance;
- staff involved in APL are conversant with the guiding principles and have themselves developed the skills to make a reliable assessment of capabilities reflected within the portfolio.

Most individuals and organizations who take APL seriously will know that it is not a soft option. It raises issues of capability in resourcing, staff development, quality assurance, equal opportunity – to name just a few. Above all, if APL is to facilitate student access to HE programmes rather than hinder or frustrate them, then the student's own capability to successfully claim credit for prior learning will need to be addressed organizationally, perhaps through a 'making your experience count' (MYEC) module. This can be used not only to discuss ground rules or expectations from both sides (organization and student) but also to explore and clarify portfolio issues such as:

- the nature of evidence;
- assessment criteria and issues of verification of evidence, ie, authenticity, currency, sufficiency, directness, reliability and breadth.

The nature of evidence

Evidence of capability can be verified using a variety of strategies such as the following.

Written tests

Written tests are often used to assess knowledge that cannot be inferred from other assessment techniques. Indeed written tests, especially unseen written tests, may also be used for their perceived authenticity and economy.

Demonstration/simulation

Some students may welcome an opportunity to substantiate their capabilities by demonstration. The main issue is to ensure that the demonstration is both relevant to the capability in question and that the demonstration is a valid method of verification.

Assignments

Sometimes, an assessor will review a candidate's APL portfolio and ask for additional information. This information can be in the form of a specific assignment or task relevant to the goals of both the institution and the candidate.

Viva voce

The APL interview can provide the assessor with ways of checking not only the authenticity of the evidence but also its currency and sufficiency. Notwithstanding the cost and other manpower issues, offering each candidate a face-to-face APL interview (viva voce) is thought to be good practice.

Product evaluation

This is what the Open University[3] referred to as direct evidence of prior achievement. This often includes any authentic products which can substantiate claimed prior learning. Candidates should be given clear examples of the range of products that are accepted as direct evidence.

Implicit in the nature of evidence are issues of:

- authenticity: that the applicant actually did what is claimed in the portfolio;
- currency: that up-to-date knowledge is evident;
- sufficiency: that the assessor knows and judges the appropriateness and quantity of evidence;

- directness: that the focus of the learning was specific or sharp and not diffuse or non-specific;
- reliability: that the assessment can be repeated with the same outcome;
- breadth: that the learning was broad enough to make wider considerations or extrapolations about subsequent knowledge and skills.

Given the issues highlighted above and the centrality of APL to the philosophy of modularization, the credit accumulation and transfer scheme (CATS) and Higher Education for Capability (HEC) movement, it is logical to suggest a case for three capabilities as outlined in the capability triangle. These three capabilities may be expanded in the following ways.

Capable organization

In order to effectively operate APL, the research-based index highlighted that it demanded that the organization perceived APL as an integrated element within its function rather than an 'add on' activity undertaken by a small number of staff. In consequence it necessitates that a regulatory framework is established, appropriate resources identified and account of APL is taken within corporate planning processes – in essence, that the organizational framework is capable of ensuring efficient, effective and quality-based APL operations.

Capable staff

Related to the notion of capable organization is the organization, perception and commitment to the development of capable staff. Staff must be adequately prepared to meet the demands of the APL process in that they appreciate the principles, and have skills to facilitate and counsel students who wish to demonstrate their capability through APL portfolios. This requires a structured development plan appropriate for each member of staff.

Capable student

The construction of an APL portfolio has its own unique demands and capabilities which focus upon the student's ability systematically to reflect on past experience, identify learning and provide evidence for the learning.

Conclusion

Although its seems obvious on reflection that APL is pertinent to HEC, the capability triangle and some of the issues raised within this chapter will require commitment and strategic planning. The capability triangle has demonstrated the intimate relationship and the interdependence there is with regard to students, staff and the organization. With the review of quality in HE and the increased access to HE, APL will have to become more and more an agenda item for most institutions of further and higher education.

References

1. Nyatanga, L and Fox, J L (1992) 'Good Practice in the Accreditation of Prior Learning', report of the research project: November 1990–June 1992, sponsored by the Midland Consortium for Credit Accumulation and Transfer (MIDCAT). Unpublished.
2. Miller, M R and Daloz, L A (1989) 'Assessment of Prior Learning: good practices assure congruity between work and education', *Equity and Excellence*, 24, 3, pp. 30–34.
3. Open University (1990) *Accrediting Prior Learning: a training pack for advisors and assessors*, The Open University, Buckingham.
4. Burnett, G D (1985) 'Giving credit where credit is due: evaluating experiential learning in the liberal arts', *Innovative Higher Education*, 10, 1, pp. 43–54.
5. Evans, N (1988) *The Assessment of Prior Experiential Learning*, CNAA Development Services Publication 17, London.

Chapter Six

Portfolio Development for National Vocational Qualifications

Howard Foster

Introduction

This chapter sets out to explain the role of portfolios in National Vocational Qualifications and to discuss the effect they may have on higher education, particularly in preparing students for employment.

This chapter refers mainly to the NVQ in management at levels 4 and 5, and the standards for the NVQ produced and marketed under the name Management Charter Initiative (MCI). Our experience is derived from a pilot programme for NVQ in management for 27 university staff, funded by Enterprise in Higher Education, which is only part completed. The objectives of the programme are:

- to develop the management skills of staff;
- to enable staff to gain experience in competence-based learning and assessment;
- to enable the university to gain experience in NVQs with the intention of providing a commercial service to employers.

The staff volunteering to take part in the pilot come from all sections of the university:

	NVQ4	NVQ5
Academic staff	8	2
Administrative staff	13	4

Most are not classed as managers, but have management as part of their job (eg, course leader).

NVQ portfolios

The development and assessment process for the pilot scheme for NVQ being used by the University of Huddersfield is essentially an APL process with candidates assembling a portfolio of evidence to demonstrate competence against the elements of the standard.

The evidence comes from the workplace. The great majority of it is in the form of documents generated during the candidates' normal day-to-day activities. Very little evidence needs to be produced specially for the portfolio. However, candidates do have to write a narrative which explains to the assessor how the evidence matches the standard. In other words, it is the candidates' responsibility to link evidence to standard, not the assessors' to search for it. A single piece of evidence can often demonstrate competence in a number of elements.

Evidence for NVQs in management can take a very wide range of forms including memos, letters, flipcharts and minutes of meetings. Even the 'back of an envelope' may suffice.

Portfolios as a means of development

If NVQs simply enabled candidates to receive credit for existing competence then they would have very limited value. Their real value is as a tool for self-development. When candidates collect evidence for an element of the standard then they will find one of the following:

- they are competent in that element and already have the evidence available;
- they are competent, but need to collect evidence to demonstrate it;
- they are not yet competent but can improve their skills themselves now they know what a good manager should do, and practice them at work, eventually generating evidence of competence;
- they are not yet competent and have no opportunity to learn how to become competent in their workplace. Eventually we will develop and offer to future candidates learning modules which will create a learning situation outside the workplace where they can develop and evidence competence.

Note that in all cases the end result is a portfolio containing evidence of competence. The NVQ process can be thought of entirely as accreditation of prior learning – prior, that is, to the assessment.

It is the third category of candidate which reveals the true value of the NVQ process. Given a standard and asked to gather evidence in a portfolio, candidates will develop themselves. Even those people who are already competent to the minimum standard required will use the standard to try to achieve excellence in their performance. For practitioners, the fourth category of candidate is not nearly as common as you might expect.

Portfolio development groups

Candidates are assigned to portfolio development groups at the beginning of the process. They meet about once a month and mutually support each other. The candidates organize the meetings and decide on structure and responsibilities. A trained adviser attends to offer support and advice, and is available at other times to talk to individuals. The experience at the University of Huddersfield and elsewhere is that candidates require very little hand-holding after the initial stages.

Assessment of portfolios

The assessment of portfolios is undertaken by trained assessors. They work through the portfolio using the candidate's narrative, verifying what is essentially a self-assessment process. They always interview the candidates to ask for further clarification. In the case of NVQ 4 in management, candidates can be assessed in one or all of nine units, but they must be successful in all nine before achieving the NVQ.

The place of NVQs in higher education

NVQs competences may be only a minor part of HE qualifications, such as degrees, but their significance should be considerable since they relate directly to employment. The ability of students to acquire NVQ competences while on work placement, or through simulation, could increase the attraction of the course to potential students, and the attraction of graduates to employers.

However, the portfolio approach of accumulating evidence against standards can be adopted for the whole of a course. The standards would be in the more general form of learning outcomes rather than competences. Evidence could include examination results, but would be much broader and therefore it would open up the opportunity for the most appropriate form of evidence to be presented. The principle that underlies NVQ, that the qualification is independent of the method of learning, is fundamentally different from much existing HE provision and requires a complete re-framing of how we look at learning in universities.

SECTION 2:
RECORDS OF ACHIEVEMENT AS A VEHICLE FOR EMPOWERING THE LEARNER

Introduction

The issues of empowerment and ownership lie at the heart of the Record of Achievement movement. Implicit in these are the issues of relevance and responsibility. Giving students the chance to be responsible and accountable for their own learning prepares them for effective performance in their personal and working lives, enhances their commitment to their studies, promotes deeper understanding and builds confidence on their ability to learn.

Ros McCulloch's chapter gives us a fascinating account of two EHE-funded projects, one based in a chemistry department, the other in a politics department, where there were attempts to introduce a process of target setting, recording and reviewing. McCulloch compares and contrasts the privacy and individual autonomy with group working and communication skills in the two domains.

Lesley Cooke and Maggie Taylor explore the issues surrounding student-centred approaches to learning, and examine some of the tensions between 'process' and 'product' as well as between the needs of the student and those of the institution. They pose fundamental questions about the purposes of RoAs, consider the current ethos of HE institutions and discuss the moral issues of freedom and responsibility.

Chapter Seven

Some Institutional and Practical Implications of Introducing Records of Achievement

Ros McCulloch

RoA: the context

This chapter draws upon two recent studies, as well as some additional material, in order to explore some of the issues that underlie the introduction of Record of Achievement processes into HE schemes of study.

Teachers and careers officers in HE have become accustomed to graduate recruitment agencies and employers asserting that what is looked for in new recruits is not just a knowledge base but also personal and organizational skills, eg, the ability to get on with others, work in a team, accept the leadership of others, accept responsibility and leadership roles oneself, schedule realistically, complete tasks on time and present them appropriately.

By giving students opportunities to record and review progress, the RoA is seen as a vehicle for the development of these competences.

The first point to make here is that these are two separate notions – there is no necessary link between keeping a record and reviewing it periodically, and the development of any of these skills. Equally, a record could be concerned with only some of these skills, depending on the particular course of study. For example, would 'working in a team' be relevant in a highly competitive situation where the person who came out on top was the one with the most knowledge? You can imagine his or her personal progress diary: Monday: got to the library before anyone else and took out all the books for the next assignment (there are two copies of each so I staggered out with 24 books in all!) Tuesday: skipped the seminar as I'm the only one who's had a chance to do any reading and I might have had to share what I know. Wednesday – Thursday: wrote my assignment and handed it in to my tutor. The following Friday: got my assignment back – as I expected I got a really good grade as no one else has been able to read the books. I'll take them back to the library tomorrow and pay the fine for keeping them beyond the short-loan period.

I won't labour this point any further, as the meaning is clear enough – the kind of RoA you come up with will depend on the culture (including the aims and learning style) of the course itself and, if you do want your RoA to reflect skills of group work and interpersonal cooperation, these have to be an integral part of that course. It's probably no accident that most of the development in RoA processes in HE has been in those courses which most approximate to the work situation itself – placements, sandwich courses and focused professional development courses like teacher training and engineering. You could move back along a continuum, with courses emphasizing a strong vocational element and significant amounts of practical group work at one end (eg, science courses, nursing courses) through to liberal arts courses at the other extreme, where the model has predominantly been that of the private pursuit of knowledge developed in a mainly private way and for its own sake. For courses at this end of the continuum, there has been little development of RoAs, students characteristically arguing that they know how they're doing from the grades they get and that self-reviewing processes are unnecessary. What such students have done in fact is accept the 'private ownership of knowledge' model, relying largely on their tutors as gatekeepers of that knowledge to let them know how they're getting on. This passive/dependency relationship will be further discussed later.

The project

Between January and June 1992 I worked with staff and students in two institutions and on two courses chosen precisely because they reflected just the kind of vocational/liberal split outlined above. The Enterprise-funded project investigated the feasibility of introducing RoA processes into first-year undergraduate courses: in one case a chemistry HND course in a polytechnic, and in the other a single-subject politics course at a university. I shall describe briefly the work, and use the results to develop further the general point made above. I shall conclude by offering some further suggestions about the introduction of RoAs into HE.

First, the project itself. Ideally, recording and self-assessment processes should begin at the start of any course of study, but this was not possible (due to the timing of funding) so each department decided on a questionnaire in which each student would be asked to voice satisfactions and concerns about the first four months of the course, and assess her or his performance in group work, tutorial participation and study skills. Following completion of the questionnaire there would be a one-to-one progress tutorial with a tutor, during which an action plan for the student would be negotiated. It was very important that this plan was seen as flexible and department-led: the tutors with whom I was working were free to adapt it as the work went on, in any way they chose. And indeed, the routes taken diverged very soon after the start of the project. Chemistry felt no inhibitions about asking students to identify themselves on the questionnaire, and went on to use each student's questionnaire as the basis for her or his progress tutorial. Politics, on the other hand, felt that questionnaires should be anonymous and then, after much discussion, decided that a one-to-one progress tutorial would be seen as intrusive by the student, and opted for a different response. The departments themselves appear to reflect the group/individual split implied by the hypothesis I set out at the beginning of this presentation, a feature emphasized by the structure of the two courses: chemistry students are frequently assessed in phase tests, and BTEC also demands that they address certain core skills; these students have ample opportunity to check their progress, work together in laboratory work and are required to make presentations. Politics students, on the other hand, though required to submit essays during the year, are only definitively tested by end-of-session examinations; their course makes no formal demands for skills of communication, presentation or group work, nor is any student obliged to speak in seminars. It is thus easier for such a student's progress to be an entirely private matter to which only she or he and the tutor are privy (with the obvious corollary that each student may well think that everyone else is doing much better!).

Clearly, the RoA was going to be easier to integrate into the the HND chemistry course: such processes as short-term target setting could be accommodated with less strain, with communications/group work elements fitting naturally into the total structure. For the politics students the processes are going to seem more remote. Courses that fall between the 'more strongly vocational' and the 'more pure' will accommodate themselves more or less naturally to RoA depending on institutional ethos and assessment patterns. I use 'naturally' deliberately, for, if an RoA, seen as any kind of formative document that involves regular review and self-assessment, is felt to be advisable, then style of course delivery and accompanying teaching and learning processes can be altered.

Student responses and the issue of reciprocity

I want now to introduce another element: that of reciprocity. Each department with which I was working laid itself on the line to some extent when it asked its students how they felt about the course so far (each was relieved to find a satisfied constituency). In asking students to voice their opinions (about course content and the integration of lectures and tutorials) the departments created at least the expectation that any concerns might be met. It seems to me that this is entirely proper whether or not a department has sought students' views: although RoA processes stress the taking of responsibility by the individual for her or his own learning, we, as providers, need to ensure that we make the opportunities for gaining that learning as comprehensive, effective and supportive as possible. Furthermore, RoAs are going to highlight areas in which this support might be improved, simply because students are recording their progress on a number of fronts.

The project's work with the chemistry department brought this out in striking ways. As a result of the self-assessment part of the questionnaire, a number of issues of concern to students emerged that would not have been seen as part of 'normal' course content: communications, planning, study skills, revision techniques, group-work skills and so on. The polytechnic offers 'remedial' help with study skills, but these students did not, in fact, see themselves as 'failing' – they just felt they needed to improve in certain areas. One wonders anyway just how much of this skill acquisition is 'remedial'. After all, which of us was born knowing how to plan, structure a logical argument and take notes effectively while listening to a lecture? There are implications here for course design – the broad range of core competences, far from being outwith 'normal' course content, need to be perceived by the students as an integral part of the course. The provision of such resources is part of giving HE students full opportunity to maximize their effectiveness, and they need to be 'naturalised' on to courses. Furthermore, there were some interesting disparities between questionnaire responses and responses to the same issues when they were explored in the progress tutorial. Only 17 per cent felt they had to plan their time more effectively in the questionnaire responses, yet the number saying this in the tutorial rose to 80 per cent. Again, in the tutorial almost 50 per cent wanted to improve their communication skills (including composing and writing) whereas in the questionnaire the need appears far smaller (9 per cent wanting to improve on structuring, 4 per cent on layout.) Naturally, one cannot read simply from one mode of response to another. None the less, the size of the disparity suggests that something is going on here – it may well be that, in supportive and exploratory discussion, students do become more genuinely self-questioning and are prepared to confront issues of concern.

It seems to me, however, that this feature of the work opened up something more subtle in the student/tutor relationship. We tend to assume in an unreflecting kind of way, when we pose questions like, 'Do you need to improve in, for example, punctuality and attendance, note-taking, effective listening?', that we all have the same measure of what 'satisfactory' looks like. A moment's thought will remind us all that this may well be far from the case – our view of 'satisfactory' may well not be the same as our students', their views will not necessarily be similar to each other's. Rarely are these questions raised, until a student's failure in an assignment or examination indicates to her or him that 'satisfactory' is what it has not been. A shared sense of what we mean by 'satisfactory', 'effective', even 'participation' – in short, the vocabulary of progress and self-review – needs to be teased out in student/tutor and student/student discussion, for only then can individuals discuss their achievement and set targets. This kind of probing and circling round meanings is what did indeed go on in the progress tutorial discussions with these chemistry students, as tutor and student together worked out shared meanings and negotiated appropriate individual targets: had the students drawn up action plans simply on the basis of the questionnaire responses (or the same questions posed in a self-review document), the targets would have been very different and, I would argue, much less accurate.

In all sorts of ways, then, RoA processes entail issues of reciprocity: students need to know as soon as possible what kinds of targets and expectations tutors have of them, and tutors need to know how they can best support the full spectrum of student learning within the framework of the course itself. All this needs to be developed as an underpinning to any system of recording achievement. Less open structures begin to return us to the 'gatekeepers of knowledge' model of which I spoke earlier: such structures are not sinister, malicious or even intentional – they're just the natural consequence of the way knowledge has been imparted to our students for many generations, and the appropriate student mode is that of patient supplicant at the gate, waiting to be told if she or he is good enough to pass through.

Student needs and the institutional setting

This picture returns me to my initial hypothesis of liberal vs. vocational, and I will complete my observations on this by going back to the politics students, whom we left filling in their questionnaires anonymously and not having progress tutorials or action planning. Their responses indicated a wish for departmental support in skill areas (just as had the chemistry students) and since the department wanted to move forward with the project, we decided on a series of sharply-focused examination revision tutorials to take place three weeks before the examination period. I prepared a comprehensive booklet, customized for the politics course, covering time management, resource organization, working with others, examination rubrics and essay techniques.

As in the polytechnic case, the information that came out was striking. Only 8 per cent of questionnaire responses had indicated a wish for departmental support in 'organizing time effectively for study', yet in discussion it quickly became apparent that very few students had any kind of study timetable at all: indeed, they were quite resistant to the thought of constructing one, even with the examination period looming. This was another example of how, in discussion, disparities of definition emerge: 'having a list in my head of what needs to be covered' was counting for many as 'effective planning of my time.'

The most interesting insights, however, came during the discussion of group work. Questionnaire responses had seemed to indicate that students were fairly satisfied with their participation in tutorials, reporting 'improvements in confidence' (53 per cent), 'frequent participation in discussion' (62 per cent), with only 9 per cent indicating a wish for departmental support in 'effective participation in group work'. The picture appeared to be that of a fairly confident body of students well used to working together in a constructive way. Since self-help groups, meeting to discuss examination topics, share essays and other resources, etc., can be of especial benefit in the run-up to an examination period, I suggested that they organize these within their tutorial groups for the remaining three weeks. The students did not wish to take this up and could not be persuaded of the potential benefits of working in this way. They felt that they wouldn't be able to stick to a timetable if they tried to work together and would get disheartened because others would know more about the subject than them: a picture, in fact, of anxious, isolated students who were finding it difficult to organize themselves for concentrated study and felt insecure about their grasp of the relevant knowledge vis-à-vis their fellow students. It needs to be stressed that these students are not in any way at risk of failing; on the contrary, they are expected to pass the first-year examination hurdle with few problems, and they are keen students who are obviously enjoying their course and have good relationships with their tutors who were present during these sessions and participated in them.

A closer look at questionnaire responses began to elucidate why this resistance to collaborative work should be so marked: when asked about the relative input of tutor and student body in a tutorial, 50 per cent felt that 43 per cent of the input was accounted for by the tutor, and 37 per cent by the students. Furthermore, 26 per cent felt 'too intimidated to speak' in tutorials, and 37 per cent felt that 'discussion is dominated by others'. Tutorial groups these days are fairly large (around 10), so in fact we have a setting where relevant knowledge issues are explored, but with the tutor as the locus of knowledge transmission and interaction, with not all students necessarily participating. Yet again the passive/dependent model emerges, and it was significant that the one area of success in the revision tutorials with all groups was the suggestion that they negotiate the topics for remaining revision tutorials with their tutor rather than leave it up to their tutors to decide what they 'needed': taking that small step towards defining their own needs was as far as they wanted to go, and of course it didn't involve them in sharing their worries and anxieties with each other. What was remarkable in all this was that the students were quite happy to admit to all their insecurities in open forum, but this was in the presence of two authority figures (myself and their tutor); they weren't actually telling each other, only speaking in front of each other, and so couldn't break through into any real cooperative mode.

There is plenty of anecdotal evidence to support the view that the department with which I worked is representative of university humanities departments: caring, concerned and much involved in supporting the students, but set in an institutional ethos that emphasizes individual development within a framework of personal autonomy. For example, repeating the examination revision skills with philosophy finalists in another university brought, at first, responses similar to those of the first-year undergraduates on the issue of working together. However, as discussion proceeded with these groups, and no doubt because finals concentrate the mind wonderfully, they began to feel there might be benefits in cooperation, and these students did plan and carry out a series of self-help revision tutorials that lasted through the examination period. Their post-finals report was that the self-help meetings had been of significant benefit: indeed they wished they'd been encouraged to use this method before (note the lingering dependency!).

Conclusion

There is no doubt that RoA processes illuminate teaching and learning styles, the attitudes of tutors and students and the culture of institutions in a startlingly clear way. If the document is to be any more than a glorified report card, listing courses of study followed and examination passes, then it is a powerful tool for change. In this chapter I have advanced the view that the closer a course is to the world of work, the easier it will be to 'naturalize' the RoA on to it, though even here innovative teaching with greater in-course support for core competences may well be needed. In the case of the non-explicitly vocational, liberal arts course, there is likely to be a need for a radical re-think of the tutor/student, student/student relationship, and such courses will need to build responsibility structures into their teaching and learning styles that they have not, in the main, considered heretofore. Where the degree itself has no obvious employment outcome, the relevance of developing an RoA to take to a potential employer may well seem somewhat remote from the student's current concerns. Here we may well have to justify the RoA for these students on the additional (and equally valid and important) grounds that the development of these skills will make them better and more successful students. It has been heartening to work with a department willing to pick up the challenge and develop it, and our subsequent work in politics will build on the information gained in the project.

Chapter Eight

Maintaining the Ethos of Records of Achievement in the Higher Education Curriculum and Assessment

Lesley Cooke and Maggie Taylor

The context for recording achievement in HE at Chester College

Current records

Traditionally, student records maintained by the college registry have tended to be summative and quantitative, rather than formative and qualitative. However, recent developments within the college have encouraged us to consider the nature, format and ownership of such records. In common with all HEIs, we are addressing issues associated with access and APL. Externally-funded initiatives, such as Enterprise in Higher Education and the Learning from Experience Trust project, are challenging conventions on monitoring and assessment. Work-based learning is becoming increasingly recognized and valued in the curriculum. Now our participation in the Wigan-based Recording Achievement in Higher Education project combines with these other strands to focus attention on the need and/or desirability of a shift to more formative types of record from entry to, through to exit from, HE.

Our current types of record demonstrate the way in which change is occurring already from the purely summative, towards a 'mixed type' where summative data are extended to include qualitative statements about the student's performance, through to more open-ended formats. Current records on each graduating student would include the following:

- annual record of student performance – summative;
- module records including record of student assessment – summative and mixed;
- enterprise module assessments – mixed and open-ended;
- work-based learning, work placement contract and appraisal schedule – mixed;
- LET project assessments – summative and mixed;
- personal tutor's report – mixed;
- college reference – confidential.

There are inevitable tensions between the desire to maintain full records and the feasibility and cost-effectiveness of so doing during a period of major expansion. There is a need to consider issues of necessary and sufficient record systems for the centre, and the needs of students for timely, relevant and sufficiently detailed feedback. A culture and associated administrative system that would encourage students to take ownership of the processes of monitoring and recording their learning within and outside the curriculum is essential.

A scenario for the mid-1990s

We believe that future cohorts of students entering HE may have the understanding and skills to take ownership of the process of recording achievement. We predict the following scenario for the mid-1990s:

- an increasing number of students will be entering HE with RoAs; a small cohort initially, rising to all school-leaver entrants before the year 2000;
- students will have been using these since entry to secondary education;
- some students will have been using them from the time of entry into the school system.

These students are likely to have the following expectations for their HE experience:

- autonomy;
- joint negotiation;
- joint goal setting;
- self-assessment.

The college's responsibility?

A culture and reward structure in HE which prioritizes research before teaching or administration may not be as supportive of an RoA/HE initiative as other education sectors. The burden on academic and administrative staff in a period of significant expansion in HE may be problematic. The viability of RoA/HE depends on the extent to which ownership of the recording process can be gradually transferred to the student – the autonomous learner. This may be seen as an academic and administrative 'cop out', but it is certainly not what is intended here. This transfer must be underpinned by support for staff and students, to acquire an understanding of the processes, skills and information systems that form the institution's approach to RoA/HE. In this way, the introduction of RoA/HE may be seen as an organizational development opportunity, not just an administrative procedure.

Where does an institution start to address these issues? At Chester College, we see our present responsibility as one of maintaining the momentum and ethos of RoAs through:

- the admissions process initially;
- staff development on RoAs with admissions tutors;
- an audit of current practice and processes which might form the basis for developing a framework for an RoA/HE for this institution;
- staff and student development activities which explore partnerships in learning; student ownership of their own learning; the role of personal tutors, employers, peers and mentors in reflection upon and recording of achievement.

We can identify aspects of current practice which maintain the ethos of RoAs in a higher education setting, for example:

- monitoring and recording performance *and* achievements requires us to identify, define and make explicit the characteristics we seek to develop in our students;
- the assessment of enterprise learning raises serious questions about who is the best party to undertake the assessment. We believe that all stakeholders in the learning experience should contribute as appropriate;
- a pilot project in negotiated assignments and assessment has proved so successful that staff and students are sufficiently encouraged to extend the process to other courses in their department. The findings will be shared with other departments in the next academic year to develop a proforma which could be used college-wide;
- through student enterprise, a range of extracurricular projects are being designed and run by students, for students: set representative training, computer literacy, and community-based projects. To encourage these developments, we need to recognize and value extra-curricular learning through our recording system.

A number of paradigm shifts can be seen to be taking place within our organization. At the *institutional level*, central and departmental recording and monitoring systems are moving from quantitative to more qualitative methods. Increasingly, more explicit quality requirements are being placed on both measures and systems.

QUANTITATIVE ------------------------------------> QUALITATIVE

with QUALITY requirements on MEASURES and SYSTEMS

At the *curriculum delivery and assessment level*, course documentation is making the responsibilities of staff, student and employer/client more explicit. Learning outcomes are not only described in terms of content knowledge, but in terms of personal transferable skills. At the point of delivery, there is a shift from totally tutor-led, expertise-driven content, to collaborative, project-based group work on live, real-time projects. This changing orientation from content to process is reflected in new forms of monitoring and recording: learning contracts, criterion-referenced assessment and formative feedback derived from a number of sources.

CONTENT ---> PROCESS

SUMMATIVE--> FORMATIVE

with QUALITY requirements on MEASURES and SYSTEMS

At the *student level*, opportunities exist within and outside the curriculum that maintain the ethos of RoAs in an HEI. Curriculum developments are encouraging students to take ownership of their own learning, and to review roles and expectations within that framework. With the increasing emphasis on capability and personal transferable skills, students are developing insights into negotiating with their tutors, peers and others associated with their HE experience. Responsibility for oneself and others is a characteristic of the autonomous learner. It is this capacity for self-directed effort which is likely to be central to any real sense of ownership for RoA/HE. The shift from the passive/receptive to active/inquisitive mode is increasingly in evidence.

PASSIVE/RECEPTIVE ---------------------------> ACTIVE/INQUISITIVE

with RECOGNITION of CURRICULAR and EXTRA-CURRICULAR OUTCOMES

Concluding thoughts

In this chapter we have shared our experiences and perceptions of the potential for RoA/HE. We acknowledge that the HE sector and individual institutions need to find their own solutions to the continuation of RoAs beyond the admissions process.

We believe that this particular initiative needs to be linked to an organizational strategy for change in teaching and learning styles, and the development of autonomous learners in times of expansion and progressive underfunding. In the earliest stages opportunities exist to identify, and build on, good practices and procedures through an internal audit. From this, a programme for staff and student development should be designed and delivered to support the initiative . . . with regular evaluation of RoAs.

SECTION 3:
RECORDS OF ACHIEVEMENT IN THE DEVELOPMENT OF SKILLS

Introduction

The terms 'core skills', 'interpersonal skills', 'transferable skills' and 'personal skills' appear to be used interchangeably, to refer to the aptitudes, such as the ability to communicate, which are assumed (not necessarily correctly) to transfer from one learning context to another.

Enterprise in Higher Education (EHE) and Higher Education for Capability (HEC) have spearheaded developments in the sphere of personal skills in higher education. A manager in the former domain, Allan Hardy, sees one of its prime aims as being 'to enable students to become effective and self-directed people'. Collaboration, project work needing interpersonal, problem-solving, decision-making and communication skills are seen as vital prerequisites for life-long learning.

Capability education promotes the development of high level personal qualities and skills, to empower students to own their own personal development and achievement, and to use their higher education for the purposes of managing their own personal, educational and professional development.

Roger Harrison's chapter presents some practical ideas on how to tackle the thorny issue of assessment of personal skills and qualities. 'What exactly is being assessed? How is it assessed? Why assess at all?', are questions he raises in the context of a new Open University course, where students' portfolios are used as the vehicle for personal career development. Assessment asks for evidence that students have identified and assessed their use of core skills as they complete the course.

In the early stages of developing a university-wide RoA, Marilyn Wedgewood and Joyce Godfrey sought to develop skills which were common to all academic disciplines and which reflected those emphasized by, for example, the CBI and validating bodies. As part of the evaluation of the project, students were asked to rate each skill area in terms of its usefulness to their learning, on a scale of 1–5. A major challenge for HE, as indeed it was and still is in the school sector, lies in securing acceptance from the students that skills development is worthwhile.

Beryl Starr's contribution discusses ways in which the acquisition of professional skills, such as interviewing, can be recorded and publicized in order to ensure their credibility with staff, students and future employers. She outlines one possible solution and considers some of the benefits that a profiling system can bring to 'gently encourage a student-centred, skills-oriented approach to HE'.

The chapter by Roger Payne, David Eaton and Chris Short describes the introduction of a portfolio assessment scheme in the school of engineering at Sheffield City Polytechnic and the ways in which this was used to develop professional and personal skills and qualities needed by effective professional engineers. Finally, Roy Gregory and Lin Thorley's chapter analyses why and how student-centred RoAs were introduced on an experimental basis onto a masters in engineering course, in which students used a Personal Skills Self-development Pack.

Chapter Nine

Using Portfolios for Personal and Career Development

Roger Harrison

Introduction

Portfolios and Records of Achievement can be effective tools in enabling us to realize some of the long-term goals of continuing education, which are now increasingly a concern of higher education and of employers.

From an educational perspective those concerns can be summarized as:

- shifting the balance of power from the teacher to the learner;
- giving learners more control over the content of and the approach to learning tasks;
- placing value on the experience and knowledge which learners bring with them to new learning tasks.

From the employers' point of view there is a concern that graduate recruits are able to show evidence of a number of skills and qualities. These generally include:

- an ability to understand and take account of their own strengths and weaknesses when completing tasks or planning further learning;
- an ability to assess and carry out tasks independently and in collaboration with others;
- an ability to learn from experience and apply that learning in new contexts;
- an ability to communicate effectively in a variety of contexts.

The concerns of educationalists and employers have a good deal in common in that valuing prior experience and knowledge can lead to a deeper understanding of personal strengths and weaknesses, and taking greater control and responsibility for the content and approach to learning encourages habits of independent autonomous learning.

In selecting, planning and implementing a programme of study which is appropriate to their own goals, individual learners will be developing a set of generalizable skills which will be supportive of further learning and development in a range of contexts including education, training and work.

Introducing portfolios into the curriculum

There are two broad approaches to introducing portfolios or records of achievement into the curriculum of higher education institutions:

- to introduce them in relation to particular subject areas, so that there is a portfolio for engineering students, one for nursing studies, and so on;
- to introduce a generic portfolio linked to the overall personal and academic development of the individual student.

The Open University, through its Enterprise in Higher Education programme, has gone for this latter approach. There are two main reasons for this. First Open University courses are print-based; they have a long lead-in time while they are being produced, and a life of five to six years in presentation. Curriculum change across the university's range of courses would take a long time. We know that Open University students have a strong interest in personal growth and career development. About a third of undergraduate entrants indicate employment-related reasons for study and many more find their confidence raised and their horizons widened, leading to a reassessment of their career potential. In the professional development areas of the university's programme – health and social welfare, management, or professional development in education – the career interest is much stronger. We also know that the most important outcome which graduates report on completion of their studies is that of 'personal development'.

These provide the main reasons for introducing a new course which takes as its approach the development and use of a portfolio, and as its subject matter the personal and career development of the individual student. The title we have used is, predictably enough, 'A Portfolio Approach to Personal and Career Development'. The overall aims of the course are to:

- recognize and value past and present achievements;
- assess strengths and weaknesses;
- produce an individual development plan;
- put into operation one aspect of the plan through a 'work-based' project;
- reflect on performance.

These aims describe a process of self-assessment leading to action planning which will be familiar to anyone involved in educational guidance or careers counselling. What is more unusual is the addition of a practical project, which might be in the workplace of an employer or voluntary organization, or in a community or domestic setting, and a final self-assessment of performance and progress. The process stages students are working through as they complete the course can be mapped directly onto the four parts of the workbook, the main text of the course. The contents of the workbook can be summarized as follows.

Taking stock

Assessing one's own style of learning and approach to learning tasks.

Assessing one's own use of skills and abilities, introducing notions of category and level.

Assessing the context for personal and career development, identifying helping and hindering forces.

Assessing one's own attitudes and values in relation to personal and career development.

Assessing one's personal support network.

Planning for development

Identifying and prioritizing goals in the areas of personal, academic and career change.

Identifying and assessing strategies for achieving these goals.

Describing priority goals together with strategies for achieving them.

Taking action

Identifying a project which will contribute to the achievement of one of the student's goals.

Completing the project.

Writing up the project.

Reviewing progress

Analysing work done on the course and the project to identify what has been learned and how it has been learned.

Identifying the use of core skills and the level at which they have been used.

Identifying ways in which new learning will influence future developments.

As students progress through the workbook they will be completing a number of self-assessment and forward-planning exercises. The results of these are recorded on activity sheets in a portfolio. There are 40 activity sheets contained in a loose leaf ring binder portfolio.

Alongside the workbook is a resource book, which deals with the underpinning knowledge and information which students will need in order to place the work they are doing in the context of changes in the worlds of education, training and work. There are sections on:

- changing needs and educational concerns;
- learning outcomes;
- assessing and recording achievement;
- core skills;
- Enterprise in Higher Education;
- careers and educational guidance.

In addition, the resource book contains a skills-building section on interpersonal and communication skills.

There is an audio cassette containing two types of material to support students with their studies. First, some introductory exercises on the use of imaging and mental rehearsal in future planning, second, material which draws on the experiences of students who worked through the pilot version of this course, and which provides an accompanying commentary to the work of new students.

Finally there is a booklet, 'Notes to Project Providers', which students can pass on to an employer or mentor as a background briefing on the EHE programme, what the course is about, and what their role might be in supporting the student's project work.

Delivery and assessment

'A Portfolio Approach to Personal and Career Development' can be purchased as a free-standing pack of materials. It could be used by individuals working on their own or as part of a self-help study group. Some help and guidance can be provided to these individual pack purchasers through the EHE counsellors in each of the Open University's regional offices. The pack might be purchased by employers who wish to use this approach to staff development within a company or organization. There have already been expressions of interest in this type of use from employers, ranging from British Telecom to health authorities and national charities. The Open University is considering using the material as part of its own staff development programme. After all, if we think these processes have valuable outcomes for our students, why not also for our staff?

Assessment in the area of personal development raises some difficult questions. Some of them are: What exactly is being assessed? How is it assessed? Why assess at all? Formal assessment on this course is entirely optional. Individuals purchasing the pack can work through it on their own or with the support of others. As they do this they will be doing a great deal of self-assessment. If they wish to be assessed by the university, they must register and pay an additional fee. This entitles them to additional counselling and tutorial support, and the opportunity to submit two tutor-marked assignments. Completion of these to the standards described in the assignment booklet leads to a 'Certificate of Personal and Career Development.'

What we are assessing is the ability of students to show that they have operated the developmental process of exploring, planning, implementing and reviewing described by the workbook. Particular emphasis is placed on the ability to reflect on and learn from the prior experience identified at the exploration stage, which should then feed through into the planning stage, and from the current experience provided by the project work at the implementation stage. As they operate this developmental process, students will be using and developing a range of core transferable skills in the areas of problem solving, communication, working with others and learning to learn. In order to define explicitly what we mean by these categories of core skills, and to give an indication of level differentiation, we have drawn on recent work by SCOTVEC and NCVQ. We feel there is a congruence between core skills development and the aims of this course.

So, the assessment asks for evidence that students have identified and assessed their use of core skills as they complete this course. We are not assessing the use of core skills at a particular level using the complete SCOTVEC and NCVQ standards. What we are doing is raising awareness of the use of core skills, and their transferability to other contexts. We are introducing notions of level, criteria and evidence requirements which will facilitate students who wish to seek competence-based assessment through an APEL route.

Certification from the Open University has already been approved. However, this is currently a free-standing certificate, and we will now be investigating ways of gaining a credit rating within the undergraduate programme and within the university's professional development programmes. In addition, we will be negotiating with other awarding bodies so that students can be offered a range of options for certification either within or outside the university.

The appropriateness of assessment in this area of personal development is open to question. Technically it is not easy. The systems available are geared towards the assessment of knowledge through written work, and are not ideally suited to this new purpose. Failure is problematic and could be more acutely felt than on a more traditional academic course. However, indications are that the development of the combination of skills, knowledge and personal qualities that constitute capability is central to the purposes of higher education. If we are serious about this purpose we must also be serious about finding ways of giving credit for it within higher education courses.

Chapter Ten

The Record of Achievement as a Learning Resource for all Students

Marilyn Wedgewood and Joyce Godfrey

Background

A university-wide RoA is being developed at Sheffield University as part of the EHE programme. Its primary function is to help students become more effective, active learners and thereby take on, in a guided and effective way, their share of the responsibility for their own learning. It does this by encouraging the habit of self-reflection on learning and by action planning for improvement. The RoA itself provides a summary of 'where the student is at' by recording achievement at identified points in time, such as the end of year, semester or course.

In the initial stages of development of the RoA in 1991, surveys in departments in different and contrasting academic disciplines emphasized the need for the development of skills which were common, in spite of initial scepticism that they could be across the disciplines. These included, for example; written and oral communication skills, library and information-handling skills. These skills conform very much to the typical lists of 'enterprise skills' identified by Sheffield and other institutions involved in EHE. These in turn reflected lists of transferable skills emphasized by employers and validating authorities. The survey also revealed common concerns for intellectual and academic development and recurring comments about the 'special' or individual nature of a discipline or a subject.

Meanwhile, work in both the school, FE and HE sector on RoAs was revealing good practice approaches in making the RoA process successful.

But it was also very clear that the HE environment was different from the schools, particularly in terms of the numbers of students involved, the limited opportunities for close contact between lecturer and student, and the characteristics of the student population. Most of the HE developments were being pioneered by individual members of staff through individual courses. This work provided many valuable lessons which included:

- the need to have clearly separated formative (process) and summative (product) components;
- the particular value of the formative process;
- the importance of separating the student-owned parts from the public components;
- flexibility in approach;
- the usefulness of lists and guidance to inform the process of self-reflection; and
- the value of support.

The Record of Achievement

The challenges for us were to introduce a pilot RoA which was workable (given constraints on staff time). For example:

- acceptable in principle to all those involved;
- 'safe' for inexperienced staff and students;
- non-resource intensive;
- cost effective; and
- applicable across different disciplines.

We decided to design an RoA which was primarily student-centred, which students could use with or without a member of staff. There would be a different emphasis in each year. In the first year, the emphasis would be on transition into HE and common transferable skills, thereby helping students adapt to being a first-year university student. Emphasis in the second year would centre upon academic and intellectual development, general to all undergraduates, and on discipline-specific skills and approaches. The third year would encourage career planning and thinking about development after the degree. The university-wide RoA was being developed to link with both previous experience through the RoA process in schools, and post-university experience through the personal development and appraisal process characteristic of many large companies. We consulted widely internally and externally with, for example, staff, students, employers, staff at other academic institutions, schools, the Careers Advisory Service and the Students' Union.

Matt Hector-Taylor, who is the assistant director of the Enterprise Unit, was responsible for the final design of the first-year pilot, which consisted of three components. The first was a *reflection document*, which encouraged students to reflect on each of the following skills:

- written communication;

- information handling;
- working in groups;
- oral presentation;
- problem solving;
- using information technology;
- academic record;
- study habits.

We started to develop written support material for each of these skill areas in the form of short accessible quickstart packages, such as Painless Presentations, Simple Solutions and Grappling with Group Work. For each page in the RoA, with an identified skill, students were given questions and example comments to help them think and were asked to assess their confidence in the skill on a scale of 1–5 and write comments. This component was student-owned and the page in the book was coloured differently.

A *student statement* was the second component. For the pilot departments, the plan was for this to be a jointly agreed statement with the tutor. The statement was summative with plans for it to be completed at the middle and end of year. (Pilot departments originally intended to allocate time to discuss this with the student.) If a flexible approach is taken, the student statement does not necessarily have to be arrived at with the tutor; it could be arrived at through discussion with others such as peers, friends, parents, etc.

A *log* was the third component. This gave a factual record of activities, experiences and qualifications gained. The intention was that this could be carried forward and added to each year, so that it was a complete record at the end of the degree.

Guidance notes at the beginning of the RoA document identified, in broad terms, what the record was for, how it was organized, and how it could be used.

The RoA was made available to academic departments without further support. Six departments from different faculties had been involved in its development and agreed to make it available in their departments. Others took it on, making a total of nine. Some modified it or only used parts of it and it was used in both first and second undergraduate years and in postgraduate courses. Ideally its introduction would have been supported with a comprehensive staff and student induction and development process but in reality this was piecemeal, as the Enterprise Unit was unable to provide the necessary staffing resources at that time.

Evaluation

Method and findings

Following the appointment of an RoA manager, the pilot was evaluated in late May 1992. A questionnaire containing precoded and open-ended questions was distributed to a sample of students in the four departments still teaching their student groups. A total of 70 questionnaires were returned. This was supplemented by semi-structured interviews with small groups of students from within these departments. Staff views were collected informally. The evaluation was also informed by changes in our own thinking resulting from the pilot experience and discussion with other practitioners of RoAs.

The intention of the evaluation was to gain information on the RoA in four broad areas: its introduction; how it was used; relevance of the content areas; and its effect on the quality of student learning.

Introduction. In spite of the fact that the RoA had been introduced with little or no staff and student induction, the majority of the students were clear about how to use it. The provision of stimulus questions and sample answers in the reflective part of the record was found to be particularly helpful. What students were much less clear about was why they should use the record, what advantages they would gain and who would eventually see it.

How it was used. While most students affirmed that they had used the RoA in the way suggested in its introduction, this did not apply to its frequency of use. This varied from the recommended once per term to once only over the year or not at all. Interview feedback suggested that where students perceived academic staff as valuing the record they were more likely to use it frequently. Student suggestions on how to increase the value of the record included a course time allowance for its completion and closer integration of its contents, with tutorial feedback on course work where this did not already exist.

Relevance of content areas. Students were asked to rate each skill area for its appropriateness to their learning needs on a scale from 1, not appropriate, to 5, very appropriate. Of the areas in the record, the skill felt to be most useful (83 per cent) was oral presentations, followed by problem solving (63 per cent) and working in groups (55 per cent). Perhaps not unexpectedly for undergraduates (most of whom are in their first year) reflections on and recording of their employment history was considered appropriate by only 20 per cent of students. However, given the limited number of departments involved in the evaluation, it remains to be seen whether or not this ranking has wider applicability.

Effect on the quality of student learning. Indirect questions were asked which enabled us to make inferences about the value of the RoA for reflecting on personal development and learning, and influencing future learning. We found that on both questions, opinion was almost equally divided, 47 per cent suggesting an improvement and 53 per cent not.

Summary

The results of the evaluation, whilst limited in scope, provided sufficiently clear indications of the actions needed to make the RoA of greater use to a wider audience:

• there is a need for both student and staff development;

- students need to be convinced that the record will help them. Its potential benefits, both intrinsic and extrinsic, must be clearly spelt out if motivation is to be secured and sustained;
- written support materials are required to help students to develop the skills and qualities in the record;
- human support is essential if students are not to be left to struggle and at times flounder;
- the areas to be included in the first-year record will need to be reviewed, especially as we move towards developing a second-year record.

Action proposed

In the next academic year, one of the Enterprise Unit staff will manage the RoA project more rigorously. Joyce Godfrey will work closely with individual departments to provide:

- student induction;
- staff and student development;
- continuing support;
- different ways of implementing the RoA to match departmental circumstances.

Work will continue on the first-, second- and third-year record. A modified first-year RoA will continue in pilot departments in the academic year 1992/93. An RoA is being developed for medical undergraduates, which will go beyond the generic record to include professional areas throughout their course. Similarly, clinical dentistry will be using an RoA for undergraduates' clinical experience and an RoA for masters-level students in mechanical and production engineering as planned. The second-year record is currently being developed for introduction into a limited number of pilot departments during the 1992/93 academic year.

Conclusion

The RoA is only part of a comprehensive programme of student development within the EHE initiative. This programme initiates, supports and encourages a set of wide-ranging curricular and extra curricular activities, which collectively aim to help students to be active, independent and reflective learners. Parallel to this is a comprehensive programme of staff development, which is helping academic staff to become more skilled in a variety of approaches for course design and delivery. This initial work is helping to make explicit that which is implicit in courses and thereby help clarify for students the direction in which they should be developing as they progress through their university course. One major challenge for the future is to gain widespread acceptance from the students of its value. Not only will it draw attention to skill development and recognize achievement, it will also help students reflect on learning as a habit and increase self-awareness and understanding. It will help students learn how to learn.

Chapter Eleven

Profiling and Assessment of Professional and Personal Transferable Skills Acquired by Students on a BSc Honours Course in Psychology

Beryl Starr

For several years, in the psychology division at the University of Hertfordshire, we have been teaching students certain professional and personal/transferable skills as part of the BSc Psychology Honours Degree scheme. This 'skills' approach is embodied within the aims of the scheme, which are listed below.

A graduate of the scheme should possess the following attributes –

- A thorough knowledge of psychology, where psychology is defined as the scientific study of mental processes. The coverage of the subject, although broad, will be acquired through concentration on a selection of 'active' topics.
- The ability to think like a psychologist; to question, to be critical and to be creative in ways appropriate to the subject.
- The ability to communicate using spoken and written language and the formats used by psychologists.
- An ability to apply psychological techniques and an understanding of their limitations. This will necessitate an understanding of the scientific method and a thorough grasp of experimental design and analysis.

- The ability to undertake original scientific research using investigative skills appropriate to the laboratory and to research in the real world.
- The graduate should be equipped with the necessary background for professional training. This will include basic training in some professional skills, along with an appreciation of relevant ethical considerations.
- The graduate should be equipped with global skills that will make them attractive to employers.
- The graduate should become a more rounded, tolerant and mature human being with an appreciation that human behaviour can be viewed from many different angles and each viewpoint has its own validity, methodologies and limitations.
- The ability to work and to learn independently and to possess an active and enquiring attitude to psychology so that the degree programme marks the beginning of a learning process that will continue throughout life.

Some of these skills, eg, written communication, are obviously valuable aspects of the curriculum which are tested in traditional forms of assessment. Other professional skills, eg, interviewing techniques, would not normally contribute towards degree classification. How could the acquisition of such skills be recorded and publicized so that their importance would be signalled to staff, students and future employers?

One solution we have adopted is to issue our psychology graduates with a personal profile listing the skills that they have acquired during the three years of their degree course. This project, funded by the Enterprise in Higher Education initiative in 1989, was originally aimed at helping our graduates convince prospective employers about the useful range of skills that they had attained. The impetus for the profiling notion was our frustration at the lack of knowledge about psychology and the misunderstanding of psychologists' contribution amongst the general population, alongside our confidence in the wide range of abilities of our graduates.

This chapter will briefly describe the profiling system at Hertford and then consider some of the benefits that a profiling system may bring.

Background

It is apparent that many psychology graduates do not become professional psychologists but use their degree as a passport into different occupations. Gale[1] estimated that 85 per cent, and Fletcher et al.[2] quote 75 per cent, of psychology graduates use their degree as a general degree. At Hertford we find this figure to be nearer 50 per cent, depending on how and when the information is obtained.

Since psychology is a discipline which encompasses both arts and science perspectives, its students are exposed to a wide range of skills. Hayes[3] lists the skills that are potentially fostered within psychology degrees. These include literacy, numeracy, computer literacy, interpersonal awareness, environmental awareness, problem-solving skills, information-finding skills, critical evaluation, research skills, measurement skills, perspectives, higher-order analysis and pragmatism. This is an impressive list and it would seem that psychology graduates have 'a lot to offer' prospective employers.

However, Fletcher et al.[2] show quite conclusively that employers do not have an accurate perception of psychology graduates: 'The stereotype of the psychologist is alive and well.' 'The psychologist is characterised as an all-purpose counsellor.' These misperceptions regularly ignore the 'scientific' skills acquired in a psychology degree.

It seemed from this kind of evidence that it would be useful to confront the employer, at the moment of interview, with a list of skills that the interviewee possessed. The assumption was that this would be more effective in changing perceptions than any amount of other information. Hence the notion of an individual student profile for each undergraduate was born.

The Profiling Scheme

The first stage in initiating the profiling scheme was to tease out the skills that were already contained within the degree programme and to examine how they were taught and assessed. Thereafter followed development work to introduce new skills and to make training and assessment of both old and new skills explicit. The first attempt at a student profile contained a simple list of skills acquired. Feedback from colleagues and from students, via the careers service, suggested that this was not particularly informative or very impressive. The current list of skills, cast in terms of 'competence statements', is given below.

This document lists some of the skills acquired by the above student as part of their BSc Honours Psychology. Only those skills which are potentially useful in general employment are included.

Communication
'. . . has received training and can communicate effectively in both oral and written modes.'

Interviewing
'. . . has attended a 2 day intensive residential course on interviewing skills and self presentation.'

Behavioural experiments
'. . . is equipped with the necessary techniques and is conversant with the problems involved in translating a theoretical or practical question into an empirical experiment capable of supplying an answer.'

Measuring people's opinions and behaviour
'. . . understands and is able to use two major methods of unidimensional attitude scaling and has experience in devising and administering questionnaire surveys.'

Time and task management
'. . . has successfully managed the structure, timing and execution of an independent research project involving liaison within (and beyond) the institution.

Analysing the components of tasks
'. . . has used a range of qualitative task analysis techniques to systematically evaluate a complex operation system interface.'

Computing
'. . . can use at least one type of microcomputer for wordprocessing, data analysis and presentation.'

Group work
'. . . is aware of the complexities of working within a group and has taken an active part in a successful 7 week, assessed group project.'

Teaching
'. . . was selected to teach and assess first year students in practical classes'

Statistics (some of the statements below)
level 1 '. . . has a familiarity with the concepts of statistics enabling communication with specialists in this area.'

level 2 '. . . knows how to design a research investigation and to analyse the data so as to maximise validity and economy.'

level 3 '. . . is able to apply to work situations the most advanced of the available statistical methods of data analysis.'

These skills are both taught and assessed within the current BSc Honours psychology programme. The inclusion of some of these skills in the curriculum was encouraged by the profiling scheme.

Teaching and assessment of skills

The following section contains a brief résumé of how these skills, included in the profile, are taught and assessed within the current BSc Honours psychology programme.

Communication

The ability to communicate in the written mode is extensively practised within the degree course. Different types and lengths of essays are produced within the tutorial setting and the tutor gives detailed advice and feedback. Training and assessment of the writing up of laboratory reports is an important part of the laboratory skills programme. Many kinds of report are required in different parts of the course, ranging from a traditional journal report, to an industrial report, to a poster presentation. There are sessions on oral presentation within tutorials and each student is required to give an assessed presentation to the whole tutor group. All these activities are recorded, in the first and second years of the course, and must be deemed to be of a satisfactory standard before the communication statement on the profile is awarded.

Interviewing

Most first-year students have, in previous years, attended an intensive two-day residential course on interviewing skills employing role play, video recording and feedback on performance. The main purpose of this course was to allow the new students to get to know each other. Therefore the interviewing prowess of the students was not assessed, since it would have detracted from the relaxed social atmosphere of the course. In view of this it seemed more appropriate to record that the student had simply attended the course. Students may also develop interviewing skills as part of their project or work placement.

Behavioural experiments, computing and statistics

These are the major skills acquired in the all-important methodology, design and analysis strand of the degree programme which runs through all three years of the scheme. These skills are demonstrated in the design, execution and reporting of laboratory and project work. Computing and statistics are also assessed in examinations. The levels of competence in statistics are determined by performance in the final year design and analysis examination. The practical programme followed in the first year is the same for all students. As they progress through the later years of the course the students exercise choice about which skills they acquire in relation to their career aspirations and interests.

Measuring opinions and behaviour/task analysis

These represent three pieces of work which might have particular usefulness in later employment. One of these is a six-week exercise in constructing and administering a questionnaire and analysing the results of a questionnaire survey. The second piece of work is a three-week exercise in attitude measurement. The third is a similar length exercise involving task analysis. These skills are assessed indirectly by means of a written report.

Time and task management

This year particular attention has been given to the management of aspects of running a third-year empirical project. Each third year student completes a project management folder with the stages and tasks in running the project set out. Forms are included to record discussion and action points arising from tutorials and other meetings. Liaison with technicians, statisticians, computer centre, administrative staff, outside institutions and subjects are all recorded. The completed folder is assessed separately from the written project report.

Group work

All second-year students undertake an experimental mini-project in groups of seven or eight with the guidance of a member of staff. This helps prepare them for the final year project. After seven weeks the project is presented as a poster which the group 'defends' at a poster session. At the beginning of this exercise the students have an introduction to the problems of working in groups and receive assistance in setting up the group's administrative processes. Afterwards each student rates themselves and everyone in their group on a number of dimensions relating to their contribution to the work of the group. The results from this partly determine the mark given to an individual student. From the ratings on self- and peer-assessment it is possible to identify those students who have been able to work well in a group situation and these are awarded the group work profile statement.

Teaching

At Hertford we have developed a 'proctoring' system whereby third-year students help instruct first-year students. This system has benefits for both taught and teacher alike. The third-year students who are offered this opportunity are carefully chosen and those who accept receive training and have their performance monitored. If they perform satisfactorily they are awarded the teaching profile statement.

Other skills

Other skills may also be included. Some students take courses in foreign languages. A few students are elected by their peers to represent their views on various committees. Some more specialized skills may be developed in the student's work placement. If there is objective evidence concerning the satisfactory acquisition of a skill then it may be included in the profile.

The principles of the profiling system

The profile was produced with the following principles in mind:

- The list of skills should be relatively short. Advice from industry suggested that anything longer than one side of A4 was likely to be skipped.
- The list should be individually tailored and should not contain negative statements. A list where some skills are ticked off would not be acceptable as this would be making negative statements by implication.
- Both professional skills (eg, attitude measurement and statistics) and personal/transferable skills (eg, oral communication and project management) may be included.
- Training and assessment of the skills should be explicit. This is not always the case (see interviewing skills and task analysis, above).
- There should be continuing tutorial support in relation to the profiling scheme so that the student is aware of their developing skills and may

remedy gaps in their profile. The student and their tutor should mutually agree the contents of the profile.

Benefits of the profiling system

Whether this scheme will help to educate employers about psychology remains to be seen. However, even if the original objective of the profiling scheme is not met it has had some beneficial effects which were not fully predicted at its inception.

- It has influenced the nature of our BSc Honours Psychology programme such that the teaching and assessment of skills has become more explicit. The constituent skills making up the profile are integrated naturally with different aspects of the curriculum in laboratory classes and tutorials.
- The profiling scheme has added weight to the acquisition of professional and personal/transferable skills which have been regarded, in the past, as peripheral activities.
- The profile relates to the aims of our psychology degree programme more closely than other forms of assessment.
- Students become more aware of the skills that they are acquiring. It also enables them to appreciate the links between their degree programme and future employment. This is of benefit in self-presentation and writing CVs.
- The profiling system lends itself to the prospect of individual students negotiating aspects of their course in terms of learning and assessment. In the long run it may help students to take responsibility for their progress through the course.

Conclusion

The present profiling scheme at Hertford is still in its infancy and there remains much developmental work to be done. One of the advantages of such a scheme is that it is relatively easy to introduce, in parallel with traditional methods of assessment, without immediate changes in staff approach, student attitude and to the prevailing curriculum. The scheme can then evolve gradually and enrich the student's experience whilst gently encouraging a student-centred, skills oriented approach to HE.

References

1. Gale, A (1990) 'Applying psychology to the psychology degree: pass with first class honours or miserable failure', *The Psychologist: Bulletin of the British Psychological Society*, 13, pp. 483–8.
2. Fletcher, C, Rose, D and Radford, J (1991) 'Employers' perceptions of psychology graduates', *The Psychologist: Bulletin of the British Psychological Society*, 14, pp. 434–7.
3. Hayes, N (1989) 'The skills acquired on psychology degrees', *The Psychologist: Bulletin of the British Psychological Society*, 12, pp. 238–9.

Chapter Twelve

Using Portfolios to Record Progress and Assess Achievement

Roger Payne, David Eaton and Chris Short

Background

In 1988 the Engineering Council[1] invited polytechnics and universities to put forward proposals to run a new type of broad-based, integrated engineering degree course which would be more attractive to students, more attuned to the needs of industry, and better at preparing engineers to be managers and innovators.

Sheffield Hallam University is one of six institutions which have received Department of Trade and Industry funding and our BEng (Hons) integrated engineering course enrolled its first students in October 1990. The major innovatory aspect of the course is the integration provided by linked project work and assignments centred on a 'ghost company' (a fictitious organization in the automotive components industry), and the use of a portfolio as a means of assessment (contributing 25 per cent of the final degree mark).

The portfolio scheme

The portfolio is seen as a means of supporting development and assessing achievement in areas of technical, professional and personal competence not necessarily covered by more traditional forms of teaching and assessment.

Although an outline of the scheme was set out in the initial course document much detail has been added during the later stages of planning, in preparation for accreditation (the course is accredited by the Institutions of Mechanical Engineers and Electrical Engineers) and it continues to evolve. This process involves the trialling of materials with the first cohort of students and is helped by regular breakfast meetings of core staff where all aspects of the course are discussed.

After the first year when five class sessions and two individual tutorials were run with the pilot course, it was decided to introduce a wider formal programme. This Professional and Personal Development (PPD) programme would not only support students on the BEng (Hons) integrated engineering course in gathering material for their portfolios, but would be introduced for all first year courses (over 300 students per year) in the school of engineering.

The PPD programme aims not only to develop a range of study, personal and communication skills but to increase personal support for students at a time when larger class sizes and other pressures on staff time were resulting in less individual work with students and there was concern about the effectiveness of the personal tutorial system. The programme is planned to run throughout all years of students' courses and is outlined below.

The Professional and Personal Development (PPD) programme

Aims

The aims of the PPD programme are:

1. to help you become aware of your professional and personal development and needs;
2. to assist you in the development during your course of the professional and personal skills and qualities needed by effective professional engineers;
3. to provide evidence of your professional and personal development and achievements.

Objectives

The programme runs throughout the course with the following objectives:

Year 1: to introduce you to the course, the school, the polytechnic and the Sheffield area
- to develop effective study and learning skills
- to develop interpersonal and communication skills
- to develop self-assessment and self-development skills.

Year 2: (in addition to above)
- to support you in preparing for and obtaining suitable training placements/periods of work experience
- to develop relevant skills so that you are able to contribute as an effective member of staff in placements/periods of work experience.

Year 2/3   (HND), Year 3 (degree) (in cooperation with employing or other organizations)
- to support you in your continuing professional development
- to develop and practise specific work skills
- to focus on initial career/job choice.

Year 3   (HND), Year 4 (degree)
- to review and evaluate work and professional experience
- to support you in gathering information, making decisions, applying for jobs, preparing for work or making other arrangements.

Throughout the course
- to help you gather, evaluate, review and present relevant material for your portfolio.

The scheme is underpinned by a *self-profiling workbook*, a development of earlier versions used in Sheffield City Polytechnic.[2] There are weekly one hour *class sessions*, covering such areas as effective note taking, time management and revision and examination techniques. These are in groups of 15–20 led by PPD tutors who are staff from the school of engineering. From work done in these sessions, elsewhere in their courses or extra-curricular activities, students build up *portfolios* of materials which demonstrate competence and personal achievement in a range of areas. For students on the integrated engineering degree course much of the material in their ghost company assignments is relevant because work is often done in groups and involves skills such as problem solving, oral presentation and group leadership. For students on the other courses, opportunities to practise and develop skills exist, but as more staff and students become involved in the programme it is hoped that more technical assignments will be set with PPD in mind.

Two or three times over the year students review their progress individually with their PPD tutor. In these 10–20 minute sessions students' own self-assessments are compared with staff comments for academic units and their portfolios reviewed. As an interim arrangement a mark relating to diligence and effort in work during PPD sessions and on the portfolio will contribute to the coursework requirement for Year 1.

The first BEng (Hons) integrated engineering students will graduate in 1994. For them, presentation of a summary portfolio will contribute 25 per cent of the final degree mark. Guidelines agreed with the first cohort of students are that portfolios:

- may focus on particular employment areas to reflect the interest of the student;
- should focus on non-examined areas;
- should indicate breadth of interest, experience and highest levels of achievement;
- should relate to the roles and responsibilities of professional engineers.[3]

Progress so far

Students have generally been enthusiastic once they have understood the scheme. The first group of 15 BEng (Hons) integrated engineering students who are now completing their second year, appear to appreciate being consulted frequently and having their comments and ideas incorporated into redrafted material.

For the 300 students who are just completing their first year of the programme there have been the advantages that staff and students have got to know each other more quickly and small problems have often been dealt with before they became serious. Students have also had the opportunity to identify their strengths and weaknesses and to develop personal action plans for their future development. For the 15 staff involved, PPD sessions have often required them to operate in ways which were new to them, adopting the role of facilitator rather than teacher, and students taking more ownership of the learning process. Staff from the Polytechnic's Personal Skills and Qualities (PSQ) project have been involved in running workshops, joint teaching and writing material to support staff in developing these new teaching skills.

Because no examples of relevant portfolios were available, five second-year integrated engineering students were interviewed and material they had produced in their first year was put together to show a possible format for portfolios and the type of evidence required. This process also had the advantage that the second-year integrated engineering student group improved their 'portfolio skills'. These sample portfolios were then used in class sessions with first-year students. The resulting first-year portfolios include some which are similar to the examples, ie, arranged in sections to show evidence for each skill area. The box below shows part of the checklist issued to students.

School of Engineering, Professional and Personal Development Programme First Year Portfolio – Checklist – Part I

By the end of Year 1 you should have achieved the relevant objectives outlined in Section 1 of the Workbook and your portfolio should show evidence of this. The table below gives an outline of what we expect, but we want you to have your *own ideas*.

Other portfolios are more idiosyncratic and many include evidence of past achievements and activities outside the polytechnic.

Assessment of such material is a major issue: staff generally feel that students should be rewarded by marks for work they have done, and that work which is not assessed is not taken seriously. On the other hand, there is the need to treat portfolios as a means of checking and developing a range of skills and so a single mark is inappropriate.

For integrated engineering students this is less of a problem because they know that a significant proportion of the final degree mark will depend on the final portfolio; such skill development is therefore seen as important. For students on other courses where portfolio assessment is only at the planning stage this is more of a peripheral activity.

The future

The first year PPD programme is being substantially revised for 1992/93, and a PPD programme is being drafted for the second year of all courses. Major changes will attempt to link PPD areas more closely with technical course units and the PPD and BTEC Common Skills programme for HND courses will effectively be merged.

In the longer term, portfolios will become a major assessment tool within all courses in the school, particularly relating to the assessment of work-based and prior experiential learning within a proposed 2+2 structure for degree courses.

References

1. Engineering Council (1988) *An Integrated Engineering Degree Programme*, Consultative Document, EC, London.
2. PSQ Project (1990) *Personal and Professional Portfolios*, Sheffield City Polytechnic (now Sheffield Hallam University).
3. Engineering Council (1990) *Roles and Responsibilities of a Professional Engineer*, EC, London.

Chapter Thirteen

Developing Student-centred Records of Achievement on an M.Eng Course

Roy Gregory and Lin Thorley

Introduction

The use of Records of Achievement is still relatively uncommon in HE engineering courses. While their benefits are now becoming well recognized there are still difficult and unfamiliar choices surrounding their implementation. This chapter describes the reasons why and the context in which student-centred RoAs have been introduced on an experimental basis to a Masters in Engineering (M Eng.) course at the University of Hertfordshire.

Context

The M Eng. students are recruited by selection from existing third-year B Eng. students. To gain the M Eng., students do an additional two semesters of study, the aim being to broaden their engineering education. The curriculum for these semesters includes European studies, business and management and management skills development modules. These students come from sandwich courses and have already spent some time in industry, thus making them relatively informed in their approach.

The management skills development module is unlike anything these students have done before, especially in that it gives much greater responsibility to the learner. It involves student-centred and experiential learning methods, with a strong emphasis on self-assessment and reflection. As part of this, RoAs were introduced this year for the first time.

The course includes a number of short exercises and two substantial projects. For one of the projects, students set up a business; for the other, pairs of students design and run science-based activities for junior school children. The presentation to the bank manager, the subsequent interview and the management of the activity with the school children are all new and challenging experiences for the group.

Throughout the course students are required to self- and peer-assess a variety of skills. The reflection and change process is facilitated by using various proformas (developed as part of the course) and also by the way exercises are set up and used. For example, groups of students make a video based on the school project, to be used as an introduction to it for next year's students. Students decide the assessment criteria for this. Reflection and learning based on all experiences and feedback are encouraged throughout.

Personal Skills Self-development Pack

This year a Personal Skills Self-development Pack was introduced as part of the course. The pack is based on the idea of a developmental profile. It is designed to be used independently and to be tutor-free, so that students have complete autonomy over how and which skills they develop. An initial questionnaire helps students diagnose their skills needs by asking them how important they think it is that they should possess a particular skill, and the extent to which they feel they do already possess that skill. The pack sets out a process that students can work by in order to develop their skills. The majority of students did well with the pack, several producing outstanding work. A small number, however, found the whole approach difficult and seemed to find skills development 'another language'.

Recording their achievement

During the process of skills development, students are constantly required to reflect and self-assess their progress. Course structure ensures that they have good records of their achievements and reflections at all stages. Towards the end of the semester this year's students were asked to produce their own final summary of their achievement on one page of A4, designed by themselves. In effect, this was to be a self-portrayal document, the single page restricting information and requiring selection of the content and choice in the way in which they wished to present themselves. The exercise encouraged overall self-evaluation and gave them another opportunity to think about their strengths and weaknesses as they ended their module. It also fitted with the student-centred flavour of the course.

Records of achievement were not only new to the students, but it was also the first time we as tutors had used them. Using examples made available by Danny Saunders of the Polytechnic of Wales, various ways were suggested to the students as starting points for self-portrayal. We noted that many of the students tended to follow similar structures to the examples, and felt that providing examples could have been restrictive. Given more time, though, students might have been more adventurous and imaginative.

The exercise produced a very lively debate among students on such issues as the relationship between this type of document and a cv, and on how the way in which the document will be used could affect its content and design. Also, what is selected in and what selected out can be very revealing, much more so than with a conventional cv or tutor-designed form. It was felt that this may not always be to the student's advantage. The exercise gave an insight into the way in which students wish to see themselves represented. It also gave us encouragement that student-centred RoAs are a practical option. It is likely that this exercise will become an assessed part of the course in future.

Outcomes

A number of students responded enthusiastically and kept their own copies of the RoA for career use, but a minority found the exercise difficult and made a minimum of effort. These tended to be the same students who found the Personal Skills Self-development Pack difficult and also found reflection and self-assessment in general hard to handle.

Our experience in other contexts suggests that while such students represent only a small minority, it is a persistent minority, and how best to approach with them the whole area of reflection, self-assessment and skills development remains a challenging question. Meanwhile, the majority of students seem to have benefited substantially from the approach described above.

A standard tutor/institution-led summary record of achievement could, and may, be developed in the future. However, this would clearly have rather different benefits from the student-centred version and would not necessarily be superior. We believe that self-portrayal documents can have unique advantages both in terms of student learning and for career use. Compared with tutor/institution-led documents, they require the student to take a more active role in learning and in self-presentation and also give them the opportunity to personally select an individual message for a potential employer.

SECTION 4:
RECORDS OF ACHIEVEMENT AND ASSESSMENT AND ACCREDITATION

Introduction

The vexed question of assessment in the realms of recording and reviewing is an unpalatable one for many. Some would argue that in schools in England and Wales the Secretary of State has assumed hitherto unimaginable control not only of the curriculum, but of its assessment. The RoA movement, born of a perceived need by teachers for a formative process to recognize, encourage and motivate pupils, has become in their view a mechanism for reporting National Curriculum test results to others, by others. Thus, a major tenet of the RoA movement's philosophy, that of ownership, has been eradicated, replaced by economic expediency and the quest for public accountability.

Others would argue that the purpose of the record dictates whether or not it requires assessment, verification and accreditation. Increasingly, it is the summative rather than formative purpose, ie, the end document of record, which is seen as being most useful, serving as a passport into the world of further and higher education and employment. Fundamental questions concerning the purposes, status, credibility, validity and reliability of RoAs are discussed in the following articles.

Katherine Cuthbert's chapter focuses on the accreditation of students' reviewing their own progress, using a newly adopted form of assessment entitled 'Evaluatory Review of Personal Learning'. This assessment affects their degree classification. Fundamental issues relating to the dilemma of assessing academic content at the expense of personal learning are raised, together with positive strategies for resolving some of the difficulties of assessing experiential learning and personal reflections, through a 'Review of Achievement'.

Karen Carter's chapter on student-led learning and self-, peer- and tutor-assessment highlights a process of empowerment which provides students with an opportunity to take full responsibility for the development of a project, from its conception to its delivery. In the process of planning, operating and evaluating the project, the students negotiate and devise their own aims and targets and assess their own personal and professional development as well as that of their peers. The collection of evidence of achievement constitutes positive feedback to students, who benefit from reflecting on their own and others' experiences and in the process turn this into learning, a process facilitated rather than directed by the tutor.

Keith Selkirk's chapter examines some of the logistical and practical problems of developing RoAs for use in assessment and outlines the uses of information technology in their production. He shares with us some specific lessons learned as well as raising some important general issues surrounding the management of change.

Helen Gladstone's chapter describes the introduction of RoAs as a vehicle for monitoring and assessing students' experience on year-long placements at Brunel University. As a recognition of the work they have completed on placement, students are awarded a Diploma of Personal and Professional Development.

Chapter Fourteen

Records of Achievement in Relation to Personal Learning

Katherine Cuthbert

This chapter examines student learning and assessment within an experientially orientated course unit called Communication and Group Behaviour, which forms part of the BA in Applied Social Studies (by independent study) at Crewe and Alsager College of Higher Education. In particular, it focuses on the implementation over this past academic year of a new contribution to the assessment of the unit – an Evaluatory Review of Personal Learning, and the challenges of achieving an appropriate balance between personal and academic learning, particularly since the Evaluatory Review is assessed and contributes towards the degree classification, being an optional replacement for a seen examination.

I'd like to thank all the students who have followed the Communication and Group Behaviour unit from whom I have learned much. Particular thanks are due the cohort of 1991/92 and those who have allowed me to quote from their personal reviews.

Aims and rationale of the unit

Before considering assessment in particular, it is important to provide some background comment on the general nature of the Communication and Group Behaviour unit. This has the overall aim of using content from humanistic and social psychology to promote awareness of reactions and responses in the social context. More specifically it is intended to enable the student to:

- develop an understanding of processes and dynamics of social interaction in the interpersonal and group situation;
- develop an understanding of models of self and identity, and the links between self processes and interpersonal interaction;

- gain a fuller appreciation of his or her own interpersonal behaviour;
- begin to link his or her understanding of research and theory in the area of group and interpersonal behaviour to real situations and problems.

The aim of the unit is not to teach social skills directly through practice and specific feedback. Rather, it is suggested that an enabling framework is more appropriate for the undergraduate teaching context and the purpose is thus to provide a supportive and facilitative context within which students can develop a stronger awareness of their own personal and social experience through making links between that experience and relevant explanatory models provided by psychology.

Syllabus content and student learning

Thus, although personal learning is an important aim of the unit, the academic syllabus content also provides an essential contribution. Three inter-related areas are examined.

1. Group structure and dynamics: eg, norms, cohesion, group goals, management of conflict, leadership.
2. Self-understanding and self-management: eg, self-identity, social feedback and comparison, self-regulation, personal well-being.
3. Interpersonal interaction and communication eg, self-presentation and disclosure, listening, non-verbal communication, assertiveness.

But how can this content be used within the unit such as to achieve the kinds of aims described above? The essential feature of the teaching learning situation is the use of experiential exercises in the context of group discussion and informed personal reflection.[1]

Use of experiential exercises

The central part of each session is taken up with an experiential exercise. Although necessarily somewhat artificial, these are designed to engage students in active social interaction where appropriate observers as well as participants contribute to the overall exercise set-up. Exercises have been chosen with the aim of being engaging and interesting in themselves, having relevance to important social and personal skill areas, and to the psychological literature. They have been selected and adapted from a number of sources, for example, Johnson and Johnson.[2]

'Debriefing' discussion

After completion of an exercise, class members discuss together their immediate reactions to the exercise to share their differing reactions and interpretations. The aim is to provide a supportive context for initial reflective review and analysis. It is important that students feel able to respond freely and honestly and this is partly aided by beginning the discussion in pairs or within small groups.[3]

Investigation of relevant literature

This literature is made available within the unit through reading and discussion, rather than through lecture presentations. At the end of the debriefing discussion an initial introduction is made to relevant literature. Students are given a set of issues which will provide an agenda for the investigation of this literature in the subsequent week. The first part of the subsequent week will be used to discuss this reading and to make further links to the exercise experience as appropriate.

Assessment

There are difficulties associated with the provision of appropriate assessment for a unit of this kind. It is important that any such assessment functions not just as a grading device but so as to promote appropriate student learning. Previously, the unit has been assessed through a course journal (pass/fail grading), three reports on specific experiential exercises, and a seen examination paper. Although the rubric for the latter emphasized that students were encouraged to support their answers through reference to relevant personal experience, there was concern that such a paper still led to a greater emphasis on academic content rather than personal learning, which is an important aim of the unit. As a reaction to this concern a new form of assessment has been introduced to provide an optional replacement for the seen examination. An examination of the nature, aims and implementation of this assessment procedure (called an Evaluatory Review of Personal Learning) and its links with records or profiles of achievement, will provide the focus for the remainder of this discussion.

What kind of RoA?

The Evaluatory Review of Personal Learning was not developed with an RoA model in view. Rather, the focus was on the provision of an assessment procedure which would provide an incentive for students to engage in reflective personal analysis of their interactional experience within the unit. If RoAs are conceived of in a rather narrow, mechanical sense, then I do not think there is much relevance to the kind of aims involved here. My conception of narrowness in this context would involve three main characteristics: first, where the review or profile is constructed very much as a 'post-hoc' activity with little dynamic interaction with prior learning; second, where the student constructs their own record but using a strong provided framework; and third, where it involves the allocation of a specific mark or grade for differential components within the overall review.

Of course, there may be circumstances or learning areas where such a narrow conception is entirely appropriate. However, I do not think that such characteristics are of benefit in relation to the encouragement of personal learning. What kind of characteristics are then desirable in this context? I would like to make the following suggestions. First, that a dynamic, analytical quality is desirable in the review. (I prefer to use the word 'review', rather than 'record' or 'profile', just because the latter tend to have static, descriptive implications.) Second, in the context of a personal review in particular, the characteristics of self-exploration and evaluation are desirable. Third, the review should be 'process orientated' in the sense that it is not something which is embarked upon at the end of the learning period but rather is worked towards during the course of the whole unit, even if the actual writing is completed at the end.

Implementation of the Evaluatory Review of Personal Learning within the Communication and Group Behaviour unit

It is all very well to describe these general characteristics in somewhat abstract terms, but what do they mean in practice, and how can their intention be described to students, so that they can get a clear understanding of what is expected of them? I want now to describe my experience of implementing the Evaluatory Review of Personal Learning over the past academic year, and to consider the outcome in terms of student performance and its evaluation.

Information provided for students

At the beginning of the year I did experience some difficulties in trying to explain to students what was expected. I provide below excerpts of the main points that were made:

Obviously you need to have some idea of what is expected of you in this assignment. However, it is difficult to be altogether precise and you will need to be able to accept something of an open-ended challenge to complete this option successfully. The following general pointers should, though, give a sufficient indication of what is expected.

- You should be prepared to discuss analytically and reflectively your behaviour, feelings and interactional responses. Examine what you have learned about yourself from the whole experience of the unit. Try to be honest and realistic in your account – don't feel that you have to be falsely modest but on the other hand don't be excessive in your claims.
- Both explicitly and implicitly you are likely to have received feedback from other members of the course unit. Be prepared to consider what you have learned from this feedback.
- You will need to be able to place this Review of Personal Learning in the theoretical context of the course unit. This does not mean that you need to have a separate 'theory section', but rather that you can show through your discussion that you have an understanding of, and can draw appropriately on, relevant theoretical content. An evaluation which was entirely atheoretical would not obtain a pass grade.
- You need not draw on all of the exercises and unit content in your Review. You can select those parts which have been most personally relevant. However, you must give some explanation of the nature of the selection you are making. Also, in order that your Review is not too narrow, you should draw upon content and exercises which derive from at least two out of the three main sections of the unit.
- You should make reference to what you have learned about yourself from the experiential exercises but you should not describe individual exercises in the specific detail which you are likely to have used within your unit journals.

- It would be appropriate, if you wished, to make reference to ways in which you have used or implemented the personal learning you have derived from the unit, beyond its boundaries. Youth and Community students, in particular, may find it useful to review and evaluate relevant experiences in the placement context. Note, however, that you will need to make links back to the framework of the unit.
- Although we are not setting a common prescribed structure for this assignment, it is clearly important that your review is well constructed and clearly written. You may well find it useful to discuss your emerging ideas for the way in which you want to structure your Review with your unit tutor before you finalise these.

Having had experience of using the Review in practice, I think that it would now be possible to provide more helpful information. In particular, I intend next year to provide more carefully integrated comment on the nature of the unit journal and the Evaluatory Review of Personal Learning.

The student response

In spite of my doubts about the information provided to students, out of a total of 33 who followed the course unit, 24 opted to complete the Evaluatory Review of Personal Learning, rather than take the seen examination paper. Of course, this demonstration of a preference for the review could just be a product of student dislike of examinations. However, in many ways the examination was a less problematic option. The paper was a seen one and was distributed to students around four weeks in advance, so that the most threatening feature of traditional examinations, their unseen character, was removed. It has not yet been possible to question students about the reasons for their choice of either option, but it is intended that this will be part of the overall monitoring of the innovation.

The quality of the reviews actually produced by the students has been generally encouraging. The majority do seem to have appreciated the kind of critical, reflective self-evaluation which was required, although, as would be expected, they varied in their ability to express this clearly and succinctly. Almost certainly the best way of giving some general impression of what was achieved is to provide a selected set of excerpts. Inevitably, these do represent some of the better examples, but at the same time there is some loss of quality resulting from making short extracts from much longer accounts.

Excerpts from evaluatory reviews of personal learning

General comment
Probably the most important part of this (unit) . . . was the state of awareness created by the discussions and task orientated exercises involved in the learning process . . .
It was like a two way thing in that to learn through relevant reading made me aware of the processes involved but this in turn continued the awareness into my personal life by applying what I saw in front of me at college to situations out in the field and to other scenarios in my life.

The construction of the course is like a jig-saw and the pieces fit together, intertwine and complement each other. They have helped me to develop a better understanding of the intricacies and problems that can arise from the mismanagement of oneself or a group. I have looked into myself as a result of the course and have found this very useful in knowing what my reactions are, or contemplating what they would be in a certain situation.

When exercises were completed, I was able to make an evaluation of my performance by means of an observer. This allowed me to examine how I had interacted with other group members or individuals. For the majority of the times I felt that the feedback was positive, which in turn was helping me to come to terms with that particular section of the course. However, if I received any negative feedback, it made me question my personal learning and understanding of the issues at hand.

Specific comment
I have learnt a lot about myself that I do not particularly like eg, my insensitivity to the effect my behaviour has upon others. In the 'tower building' exercise (which was designed to demonstrate the effectiveness of different styles of leadership), I had to assume a democratic style of leadership. I tried very hard to hold back my own ideas and encourage and make suggestions without appearing to be patronising or condescending. By being so consciously concerned about my manner and the effect that I was having upon others, made me very aware of my normal lack of regard. I normally tend to assert myself in spite of the consequences. I suppose 'autocratic' is more my style when it comes to leadership.

During an exercise relating to deviance and cohesiveness I was really shocked at my attitude towards the deviants. I felt very angry at the intrusion of these latecomers, the group norms had already been established and I excluded them from any discussion. Upon reflection I realise this could have had an adverse effect upon the group decision, insulating information, not allowing change to take place and stifling creative thought.

After the exercise a period of feedback took place during which I was severely criticised for my dominating behaviour. Susan and Margaret both put forward an opinion that I had been oppressive, especially towards women and would only respond to the men. I had thought that I was facilitating the entire group and had responded equally to all participants, but judging by their vehement protests I had discriminated against women and dominated the group. At the time of their complaints I responded in a very aggressive way – stating that if the women felt oppressed they should structure debates in future which afforded them more of a say – but looking back at my actions and my state of mind, I can now see how I would have oppressed them. A part of me feels good about that because I feel that all white people should know what it's like to be oppressed; another part of me feels sad that I oppressed women who already have to function in a patriarchal society, coping with the pressures imposed upon them by men.

In the 'life-line' exercise, my line appeared to reflect a broad, simplistic outlook on life, which contrasted quite markedly with my partner's. His line reflected a meticulous attention to life's details. In the short term/long term goals exercise, I again became aware of my 'macro' approach to life. My goals are imprecise and based upon broad notions and concepts relating to my rather hazy ideals. I was rather disconcerted by the exercise as my approach to life seemed rather irresponsible when compared to my partner's whose goals formed a logical progression, with much emphasis on long term goals. His future was something for which he had a detailed plan, and as such was something to which he was looking forward. However, I tend to live from day to day, my future by contrast is something that will 'happen to me' as I have not really planned it.

We all engage in a process of evaluating ourselves in terms of how good we are in comparison to others. Sometimes we attribute our performance to internal factors, other times to external/situational factors. Throughout this course I have learned to evaluate my own performance and be honest with myself in terms of how good I am at certain tasks. I sometimes have a tendency to attribute my successes to internal factors and my failures to external factors. This is not very productive when I am trying to evaluate my own performance. I have learned to be more realistic and not to blame my circumstances when the fault lies with me.

The feedback I received in the exercise on non-verbal communication (NVC) was very influential in terms of personal learning. The purpose of the exercise was to speak to someone who could not see you and at the same time you could not see them. I was the speaker. I found it incredibly difficult to communicate in that I felt uneasy, I desperately wanted to see what the other person was doing, in terms of movements and facial expressions. I realised from this exercise just how much emphasis I place upon NVC. I place so much emphasis upon what the other person is doing, that if I cannot see them I cannot talk to them.

My listening process has improved since I have been at college. I am now much more aware when I am listening and when I am not. Recognising that listening is not a natural ability, that it requires energy and effort has allowed me to work consciously on improving listening as a skill.

In my daily life I am often outspoken and refuse to be ignored. I never really thought of myself as an aggressive person but maybe sometimes a little over enthusiastic. The course on assertiveness made me realise that when I want to express my opinions or my point of view I can come across in a very forceful and over zealous fashion. In looking at behaviour that constitutes aggression I realised that I do act in an aggressive way.

Inherent problems

Rather than making a comprehensive evaluation of this innovation, which is probably premature at this point, I would like to examine two inherent dilemmas which revolve around the same issue – that is the achievement of an appropriate balance between personal and academic learning.

An evaluatory dilemma: personal support vs academic evaluation

There is an important and probably inescapable problem posed by the evaluatory review and which is inherent in any attempt to emphasize the importance of personal learning within an academic context. A numerical mark is allocated to the review. This is partly because of the requirement for grading within an academic unit, but also more generally because the provision of a mark signifies the value attached to a task and has motivational implications. (It would have been possible to have used a pass/ fail grading as for the unit journal.)

The problem derives from the need to provide a climate of interpersonal trust and acceptance within which personal exploration and growth is thought to be most likely to take place[4]. However, such personal support as can be provided through the interaction within the course, may be counteracted by the actuality or risk of receiving a poor mark for an assignment which involves an examination of one's own personal qualities, and which could constitute a very strong degree of personal threat. I was very conscious of this risk as I marked this first set of evaluatory reviews and tried to be particularly careful of the kind of comment made. I do not yet know how students have reacted. Some students have received their marks but none have yet had the reviews returned to them.

Balance of aims and content: personal learning vs academic content

It might be argued that the introduction of the Evaluatory Review of Personal Learning, as a replacement for the more conventional examination (at least for some students), has changed the balance of the unit so as to put an over-emphasis on personal learning to the detriment of the academic orientation of the unit. I would not accept this criticism, as I think that in this case the suggested dilemma is a false one. The academic content of the unit is important, both in itself but also because it provides an essential support for the personal learning which is being encouraged. More generally, current research and thinking about student learning, particularly that derived from the work on deep and surface processing, suggests that for effective deep learning, personal and academic understanding are closely bound up with each other.[5,6] Student comment seems to suggest that they share these perceptions, as illustrated by the following extracts from a student's journal:

On reflection, the exercises have helped enormously, mainly by encouraging my self interest in the subject matter. By experiencing processes in them, the various topics have seemed 'more real', and I am now able to recall the year's work with great comprehension and clearness – as opposed to having to learn the subject matter from texts purely, often involving inapplicable models or theory. My own interest has led to a liking of this area of social psychology, which in turn has encouraged my self motivation to work and understand, and therefore aided my learning.

Although the exercises were conducted in a somewhat unrealistic and constrained environment, they have nonetheless managed to increase personal awareness, better my communication skills, and have helped my self confidence enormously.

I feel great satisfaction in completing the course, and will remember it as an experience of relevance and enormous insight.

Overview and conclusion

As will have been evident, this is very much a review of an innovation which is still under way, and remains to be fully evaluated. However, I think that initial indications suggest that it is of benefit in its particular context and that it does provide an example of the way in which a review of achievement can contribute to the development of personal learning.

References

1. Boud, D, Keogh, R and Walker, D (1985) 'Promoting reflection in learning: A model', in Boud D, Keogh R and Walker D (eds) *Reflection: Turning experience into learning*, Kogan Page, London.
2. Johnson, D W and Johnson, F P (1990) *Joining Together: Group theory and groups skill*, 4th edn, Prentice-Hall, Englewood Cliffs, NJ.
3. Pearson, M and Smith, D (1985) 'Debriefing in experience based learning', in Boud, D *et al.* (eds) *Reflection: Turning experience into learning*, Kogan Page, London.
4. Rogers, C (1967) *On Becoming a Person: A psychotherapist's view of psychotherapy*, Constable, London.
5. Gibbs, G (1992) *Improving the Quality of Student Learning*, Technical and Education Services, Bristol.
6. Ramsden, P (1992) *Learning to Teach in Higher Education*, Routledge, London.

Chapter Fifteen

Student Empowerment Through the Recording and Reviewing Process: Theatre in Education with Student Teachers

Karen Carter

Introduction

This chapter outlines the ways in which students are required to take responsibility for their own learning and its assessment through a process of recording and reviewing. Target setting by individuals and by groups, negotiated between the individual, the group and the tutor, are central to the process. Self- and peer-assessment and student accountability require students to elicit feedback from a wide range of sources, and to record and analyse this in order to clarify their own thinking and to shape future projects. The role of the tutor is also examined.

This example of the use of the process of recording achievement in higher education is based on the work of BEd (Hons) students undertaking the second year of the degree. Drama is their chosen specialist subject and involves six hours of study per week. All students are intending primary school teachers. The year-two course is devoted entirely to work on a theatre in education project, to be undertaken in schools in the summer term and evaluated as part of their assessed work.

Student-Led learning

The work of the students focuses upon the planning, development and performance of a theatre in education piece suitable for primary-age children. The students take full responsibility for the development of the project from its conception to its delivery in school. The course involves both practical and theoretical work and contributes to the student's development at an academic level as well as at a professional level. The students are therefore provided with opportunities to enhance their skills and knowledge through a project theme and context which is selected by them.

The style and nature of the piece is decided upon by the team and background information is researched by them, in terms of both drama techniques and educational approaches. As up to four teams may be operating at any one time, a heavy emphasis is placed upon personal research, reading and reference to prior experience. The tutor's role is to complement student-led activity by providing taught inputs through lectures or on a more informal basis through discussion with the team, in order that the individual needs of the teams are met through practical and theoretical work.

Target setting

Students engage in target-setting activities at key points in the project. This activity fulfils a dual purpose. First, it informs the tutor of the needs of the group, in order that teaching input can be appropriately planned and provided. Second, it enables the students to engage in a systematic process of planning both for themselves at a personal and professional level and for the project at an educational level. The student teachers engaged in the project address their planning in terms of performance and theatrical aspects and in respect of the educational value of the experience for children. They are therefore involved in planning and target setting as both an actor and a teacher, this dual role being reflected in the performance of the piece itself in schools.

The planning, operation and evaluation of the project is undertaken with two central aims in mind. The first is concerned with achievement as an individual and the second is based upon a process of group decision making:

- *Personal/professional aims*: targets set for self-development as a student of drama and as a student teacher.
- *Educational aims*: targets set for the teaching/learning situation in which the children are involved.

The students are responsible for devising these aims and for target setting in respect of the above areas. In this way students are accountable first to themselves, second to their peer group and third to the tutor. Student accountability for planning and self-assessment thus goes beyond the demands of the formal assessment process or of the tutor; it contributes centrally to the development of the project for the individual as well as the team.

The process depends heavily upon the students' self-motivation, self-awareness and sense of responsibility and commitment to the project. The assessment criteria for the project set the framework for these demands. However, it is largely the students who shape the project and exert peer pressure in ensuring that they are met. In addition, students are provided with the opportunity to set their own targets within this framework and are able, as a result, to organize their work and the allocation of roles and responsibilities, in order to use their strengths and develop expertise in areas of weakness. Learning targets are therefore negotiated between the individual, their team and the tutor.

In engaging in the target-setting process the students are encouraged to establish criteria for success in relation to the aims set for themselves and for the children, so encouraging a consideration of the ways in which they could demonstrate achievement at the summation of the course. This is particularly useful in the context of the educational aims of the project as it enables the students to consider forms of assessment they themselves would use in establishing evidence of their success in school.

The process of planning, delivering and evaluating the learning process for the children through the project is directly transferable to work at the student's own level; in this way students are exposed to the idea of scrutinizing their own learning in a similar way. Thus whilst developing specialist knowledge and skills as students of drama, in studying theatre in education as a dramatic form, they are also able to develop an insight into the learning process itself. In this way the principles of teaching and education are explored alongside those of drama as a subject study.

Self- and peer-assessment

The course provides opportunities for self- and peer-assessment in following up progress, development and achievement in respect of the targets set by students in relation to the assessment criteria for the course and the personal aims of the student established at the outset of the project.

Students review their personal targets formatively at the end of the first term and present a written statement reflecting upon their achievement in relation to their targets. They are then asked to reflect on their written comments and decide upon action for the following two terms. The written statement is shared with the tutor and used as evidence of achievement and as a source of information regarding the planning of teaching input.

As the focus for the self-assessment activity is both personal and professional there is the opportunity to reflect upon skills associated with the theatrical aspects of the project and the emphasis upon team-work skills. Additionally, students consider aspects pertaining to their individual development as a teacher.

Group discussion and analysis are central activities to the reviewing process and to the development of meaningful evaluation in a team context. Project groups are encouraged to review regularly their progress as a team and as a result plan ahead, setting targets for the next stage of the project.

Additionally, students share their work with other groups of students (from different year groups on the course) and with other tutors, for the purposes of scrutiny and feedback. This feedback is documented by students and reflected upon as useful evaluative evidence of the performance of the team. This process also encourages students to clarify their thinking and intentions, as often they have to justify verbally their actions or approaches to their peer group. Project aims may then be changed or altered as a result of this experience.

Students are also encouraged to collect evaluative data from the schools in which they perform and are asked to devise ways of collecting evidence of their achievement in the project in relation to its educational aims. This may involve designing an observation sheet or questionnaire for the class teacher or tutor, or devising a series of questions to guide discussion with the children. Evidence from each of these participants is then collated and measured against the criteria for success established at the outset. This provides the students with a range of experiences and a wealth of information on which to base their own evaluation. The students then use this feedback as evidence to support their written evaluation of the project, which constitutes 50 per cent of the formally assessed grade for special subject drama in part one.

The assessment undertaken by students is complemented by tutor assessment using the assessment criteria defined for the practical element of the course. Time is utilized in sessions and during the practical examination, ie, the performances in schools, to provide a focus for observation. Thus both formative and summative assessment is undertaken by the tutor and recorded in the form of short written statements which are used for the tutor's own reference and discussed with students where appropriate.

At the summative stage of the project the students engage in self-assessment developed through discussion and resulting in a written statement of achievement. The structure of the written statement is closely tied in with the assessment criteria for the practical element of the course. The students address each criterion in turn, incorporating aspects of their personal aims established at the outset. In addition, students are asked to grade themselves 1–5 (low – high) on their achievement in respect of the criteria; this grading system is roughly matched to the percentage marks given for the practical element awarded by the tutor. This written statement is then shared with another member of the team and with the tutor.

This is a particularly useful form of evidence for the tutor who gains an insight into developments and achievements pertaining to individual students. The statement is used along with other evidence such as peer-assessment sheets and tutor statements in arriving at a formally assessed grade for this element of the course, which constitutes the other 50 per cent of the total marks awarded for part one.

At the same time, students are asked to work in pairs using the grading system and to assess each other's performance in relation to the criteria. These assessment sheets are then shared and students discuss the reasons for the grades they have awarded. This often provides a useful balance to students who undervalue their achievement on the self-assessment sheet.

Although some students find this difficult initially, when they share assessments responses are very positive. Affirmation of achievement from a peer seems to have a positive effect and often stimulates valuable discussion. This is particularly useful to the tutor as the peer assessor is perhaps more closely involved in the student's individual contribution than is the tutor. As a result the peer-assessment sheet provides another source of useful information to be taken into account when arriving at a grade for the practical element.

The final form of reviewing in which the students engage is as part of the reporting system for the BEd (Hons) course as a whole. Here students use their previous assessments and statements to provide an overview of their achievements on the course and engage in target setting for year three. These comments are considered by the tutor who adds a statement. Both sources of evidence are considered together and discussed with the student in a tutorial at the end of the year. This report form is stored in the student's personal file and is considered alongside report forms for other aspects of the course during a review session with the student's course adviser. This evidence is then used in compiling a summative statement of achievement in year four, which is used as the reference for employment.

The role of the tutor

A central issue raised by the development of this initiative is that, for it to be successful, there must be a willingness on the part of the tutor to hand over some of the responsibility for learning to the students. This naturally implies that the status of the student in the learning partnership is enhanced and tutors must be prepared to accept this. Implications for the teaching/learning styles adopted on such a course are wide ranging, particularly as such an approach demands flexibility of the tutor as much as it does of the students. One important requirement of valuing student ownership and contribution to the teaching and learning process is to ensure that teaching provision is tailored to meet the needs of students as they define those needs and as they emerge naturally from the process of self-assessment and recording achievement.

It is also significant that student self-evaluation activity needs to be given status within the course. The value of recording achievement as part of an ongoing process of personal and professional development can be easily justified to intending teachers; however, it is also necessary to acknowledge the usefulness of evidence provided by RoA in contributing to the assessment process. In this instance, it is the tutor who awards the grade summatively; however, this assessment is based upon a range of evidence, and student awareness that their contribution is valued needs to be developed.

Students must be given a higher profile and an elevated status in the teaching/learning partnership if we are truly to value their contribution and demonstrate our commitment to their progress and development. This may mean, in certain circumstances, having the confidence to be challenged by students who may not agree with tutor assessments and this in itself is quite an enlightening experience, especially when the student holds the key to evidence of achievement of which the tutor has no knowledge. In such cases it is the relationship which is established between tutor and student which is important, as it is vital that both parties feel they have equal rights when it comes to assessing achievement.

Evaluation

The benefits to the students of engaging in this process of recording achievement and its associated practices of target setting and action planning are perhaps best summed up in the students' own words . . .

From working in the group project I have realised how completely necessary good planning and evaluation are, especially as they are important skills for the classroom. I am beginning to be able to trust my judgment of what is necessary in a given situation, which I feel will prove invaluable to me as a teacher.

My self-confidence has increased tremendously due to the fact that I have a responsibility not just to myself but to others. I feel I am more able to accept criticism and to put forward my opinions in a less dogmatic way, allowing for discussion and open negotiation.

This approach has been particularly beneficial in giving students more self-confidence and self-motivation and it has promoted a greater sense of commitment to quality. There has been a real sense of challenge amongst the students, to which they have responded well. The emphasis upon target setting and action planning has been useful, not only in encouraging success in the project, but in highlighting the importance of these processes in a professional context, for the students as teachers.

It must be acknowledged, however, that while some students respond enthusiastically to setting their own 'goal posts' and moving them where necessary, others may find this initially quite threatening, as perhaps previous experience has taught them that it is the teacher/tutor who should lead the learning process:

The course element itself was difficult in so much as I as an individual was unsure of what was expected of me and the group in which I worked. I found the notion of the Theatre in Education project and its 'freedom' very difficult to comprehend at first, in comparison with other subjects which all seemed far too rigid and monotonous.

This type of insecurity can be overcome and in this case was, as the course progressed and the student learned to deal with this new-found freedom. Nevertheless, tutors need to be sensitive to such reactions and support students through the process of taking on more responsibility for their learning.

It would be true to say that from the tutor's perspective a major concern is encouraging quality self-assessment. The notion of developing autonomous professionals or reflective practitioners is nothing new to teacher education:

it is a philosophy which underpins everything that we do and in this context recording achievement has a central part to play in contributing to this type of development. In looking back over the period of student involvement in this initiative, it has been evident that the quality of self-reflection has improved and this has been evident in both the analysis in review sessions and in the students' self-evaluative written statements.

Student responses

Finally, it is perhaps most appropriate to consider the students' response to engaging in the RoA process, particularly as in this case their ability to be self-evaluative is in fact one of the criteria upon which they are assessed. Students range from those who have found it difficult to self-assess and record achievement, to those who feel their skills in this area have developed considerably. The comments speak for themselves; the views of all members of the group are represented.

I find self evaluation arduous, however, personal aims which I made at the start of the project I have managed to fulfil. I constantly reflected on my role in the drama which led to a continual development of my character.

I find this part quite hard to do in terms of assessing myself, however, in terms of assessing the group it was quite easy. Overall, we had no real problems as a group and I thoroughly enjoyed the experience.

Arrgh! It's hard! I have improved over the year though, I find it easier now to be reflective.

I must admit that I haven't given my personal aims too much reflection. At the beginning I was very concerned about dominating the group, however, once I realised that I was able to address this problem, I relaxed and enjoyed the whole. I feel that self evaluation is an internal process for me, something I do almost subconsciously rather than consciously.

Personally I find it very difficult to be self-evaluative and therefore as a group we arranged to get together to evaluate our work.

It is quite hard to assess yourself. I can see some development from my previous statements. I feel that my role improved very dramatically when it was performed to children, their responses helped to feed my character and reactions. We reflected and used ideas, which were there to enable me to develop my actions relating to the performance. We developed a plan of action to the extent that we set ourselves certain tasks to complete on our own – this made it easier as we all knew who was responsible for what.

Action planning was undertaken by me as an individual and as a member of the team, relating to the project as a whole. I was able to assess my own performance when rehearsing in order to generate relevant questions and contributions in the performance through my role. I tried to keep the overall aims of the project in mind and relate them, as best I could, to situations within the drama.

I have developed in my ability to assess my professional skills at team level and in my approach with the schools involved. I have begun to carefully plan my actions. On a personal level, I have become more reflective than before and now I think of ways of developing, however, I tend not to put my plans of action into motion sometimes.

I would say that I am an honest person and I would say that from my previous self-evaluation last term, I have shown the ability to develop. Although some members of the group have been distressed by my sense of humour and have thought me immature and uncommitted, I found my attitude a god send as the pressure of assignments and the project mounted. I found something very important out about myself through the project – when I am nervous I tend to giggle a lot and this can upset others – so I think in this department I need to conduct myself in a more professional way.

I think I am rather critical of myself and also tend to quieten down when others are around – this probably gives a rather negative view of my contribution.

I have been successful in assessing myself in a self-evaluative way. In theory though I probably haven't ventured as far as I could have, as my written work may not reflect all that I feel in my development. Thus the practical work has been my opportunity to demonstrate this. I think mostly my strength has been the way I have been critical of my role and the fact that it came off so successfully in performance meant my self-evaluation was beneficial to me in this area.

Chapter Sixteen

Using Information Technology for a Student-produced Record of Achievement

Keith Selkirk

Introduction

In this chapter, I aim to concentrate on those aspects of our work on Records of Achievement which are applicable to other courses, particularly undergraduate ones, and to suggest how ideas we are developing might be used by our colleagues in other institutes.

Our RoA developed initially out of the Technical and Vocational Education Initiative (TVEI) and was later supported by the Enterprise in Higher Education Initiative (EHEI). We adopted an approach which was underpinned by three guiding principles. These were: brevity, relevance and commitment.

Information Technology allowed PGCE students to develop their own RoA, using a personal disc throughout the year. Lessons learned may be summed up as having tried to move too fast, without securing the commitment of all those involved.

Records of achievement in PGCE courses

Those working in initial teacher training have had to introduce the principles of an RoA to student teachers since these students will probably be administering such records when they start teaching in schools during the following year. Such one-year courses provide an ideal opportunity for introducing RoAs into HE for two reasons. First, they are short, lasting only 36 weeks of teaching time in a single academic year. This means that a record can be set in place and completed relatively quickly; and changes can then be made for the start of the subsequent course in the following year. Second, the RoA is seen to be relevant by the students since they will be having to administer such records themselves as part of their jobs in the year following the course. It is not surprising therefore that PGCE courses have led the way in the production of RoAs in HE, and a number of approaches have been described in the proceedings of three conferences, at York,[1] at Bangor[2] and again at Bangor.[3]

Records of achievement in undergraduate courses

Many HEIs will soon be involved in the production of RoAs for all undergraduates. My own university is committed to this objective. However, very few of us have any experience of producing such records, so HE is in the peculiar position of having to learn from schools, and particularly from secondary schools, some of the expertise necessary for setting up such records: we would be very foolish indeed to neglect the accumulated wealth of experience which the schools now have. Ideas about RoAs can filter through to HE staff either through the students (who will have had no experience of their administration) or through departments of education, and in particular through the PGCE courses. This chapter has been written so that some of what we have learned in setting up our own RoA can be passed on to others in HE.

Early steps toward our PGCE RoA

The work on our PGCE RoA developed out of a TVEI project during the years 1989–91. In 1990 we adopted a cascade model in teaching some sections of the PGCE course which offered us potential for developing a new approach to the training of students in the area of assessment, including RoAs. This proved to be an exciting opportunity to start developing ideas with students. Our next step began early in 1991 with the development of staff training[4] which took the form of a carefully planned day organized by a small working group. The award of £4000 of EHE money allowed us to set our record in place during the academic year 1991/92, and we intend to make it a fundamental part of our assessment procedures in future years.

Working principles of an RoA

As a starting point for our RoA we used the Department of Education and Science Circular 8/90,[5] and in particular Annex B. This document was in turn largely based on the report of the Records of Achievement National Steering Committee,[6] commonly known as the RANSC Report.[7] More importantly, we evolved out of these a number of working principles which are summarized below.

Brevity

The need for brevity in an RoA stems from the need to avoid excess pressure on students, teaching staff, departmental administration and especially on users of the record (mainly future employers). Experience from schools suggests that few employers are likely to read in detail more than four sides of A4 paper and this was recommended in the RANSC report. The draft NRA runs to six sides of A4 but includes routine recording of schools attended and certificates obtained which might be more appropriately placed in separate documentation. This brevity might be a relief to many of us, since it suggests that we must confine what we write to absolute essentials.

Brevity does not mean adopting a checklist approach to the record in order to save space; all our instincts rebel against this. Students are not to be summed up in a checklist of tasks completed which reduces them to the lowest common denominator. Checklists are not going to be helpful to prospective employers except to reject those who will easily be rejected anyway; they do little to reveal special talents nor allow space for special additional qualities which the students may have displayed outside the mainstream of the course and do little to aid the formative aspects of the record (see below).

Even the briefest of records is going to be difficult to support administratively if it involves large amounts of paperwork, and in particular of typing. We were faced with the need to produce records which would be printed pieces of English, and which would need to be restricted in length. This consideration led us to explore the possibilities of information technology in the production of the record. I will explain how this was attempted later.

Relevance

This was less of a problem for our students and staff than it is likely to be in some undergraduate courses. It is a particular difficulty in the early stages of developing an RoA since it is seen as an extra burden by students. Perhaps the best way of tackling this problem is to face it head on. RoAs can be used directly in applying for jobs or indirectly in preparing job applications. In either case the possession of a well developed record will give the student a better prospect of obtaining a post.

Relevance to students is not the only sort of relevance however. As teachers in the HE system we need to think about relevance to ourselves. The introduction of an RoA invariably leads teachers to question the aims and achievements of their courses, and inevitably results in better appraisal of teaching in its widest sense. The production of an RoA in collaboration with a student is likely to lead to a frank and mutually supportive appraisal of the work of both student and teacher. Thus the result is, in a climate of staff appraisal and academic auditing, of relevance to our own work as well as to that of our students. These considerations merge gently into the idea of commitment.

Commitment

The RoA can be used as a powerful means of developing students' commitment to their work. It is most important to realize that assessment has both formative and summative functions. Preliminary versions of an RoA can be used formatively to set realistic aims and objectives for students and hence improve their commitment by helping them to direct their work more effectively. Thus the formative part of a record may well include a mutually agreed statement of objectives towards which the student will aim in a subsequent period and which can then be used as a marker in measuring future progress.

There is a problem about whether such formative material should be included in the final record. The danger is that employers might see stated and, as yet, unattained objectives as being negative rather than positive. It may be sensible for formative aspects of the record to be deleted in the final document which would then be a statement of positive achievements, negative points appearing only in so far as they were omitted. However, in a vocational course such as the PGCE (and one can think of several departments where similar considerations might apply: law, engineering, agriculture and medicine, for example), it is possible to be more productive than this. No vocational course can equip students fully for the complexities of jobs such as teaching, social work, nursing or architecture and there will always be a need to promote ongoing training. Any sensitive employer will be aware of this, and a positive realization by students of their further training needs, particularly in the early years of work, can be seen as part of a mature attitude of commitment to the job and an understanding that an initial training course is only the start of a career in which there should be on-going personal development. This can be of special value when taken in conjunction with the tutor's reference. The choice is one which must be made within each course, and it may be necessary to modify the decision after a few years as employers become familiar with the idea and learn to trust the information which is contained within the record.

Implementing the record within the PGCE course

There is little need to go into great detail about how we implement the record in our particular course. We do not start the record until a month into the course, about mid-October. Students have enough to do in this crucial phase of their work without giving them an additional worry. We then introduce them to the first part of their record, with the warning that they will be required to discuss it with their tutors on four further occasions. By the start of the summer term, a full negotiation with the tutor should have taken place. This includes negotiating in detail the work to be done during the term, each student having an individually tailored personal package of practical work and short courses which will make good missing earlier experiences, particularly those from teaching practice. The package is then appraised when the final document is completed at the end of the course. This not only summarizes the student's personal appraisal of what has been gained from the course, but also details the perceived needs for further professional development during the early years of a teaching career.

For the tutor with a group of 12 to 14 students, I estimate that a maximum of four days' work is needed during the year. However, about half of this takes place in any case in giving tutorial help and advice and some of this is made easier because the student has been forced to think about the tutorial before it actually takes place. The best students often have a very clear idea of what they wish to achieve.

The role of information technology

The way in which we attempted the production of a compact and well-produced record was perhaps the most innovative part of our work. Andy Pierson wrote for us a program which allowed students to develop their own RoA using a personal disc throughout the year. This could then be discussed and amended at intervals before receiving interim validation at the start of the summer term and final validation at the end of that term. Left to themselves, many students write far too much, and we dealt with this in a drastic manner. In each section of the form the amount the student could write was limited by the space available for it since the program will allow the entry no more than a prescribed amount. The finished record could then be produced on a laser printer to ensure a good quality final document. The program is currently available for both BBC and Archimedes machines since these are the ones which are in the greatest use in local schools and are as a consequence available in our computer laboratories. Validation is achieved by leaving a small space available for tutor comments (which may be in manuscript); these are to be agreed between tutor and student and signed by both.

Ownership

One point which we have not mentioned above is the problem of ownership. The finished document is clearly a very sensitive and personal one, and students will rightly be upset if improper use is made of it. We already have a situation where students read and agree on the references we write for them, but this openness could be undone if the RoA were misused. We have simply taken our line from the practice in schools where the record belongs to the student. We do not keep any copy without the student's agreement. The document is theirs to use as they think best. If the student wishes us to keep a copy of the record for them, we will be happy to do so for a reasonable period, but we do not do so on disc. This also overcomes any legal problems about keeping computer records.

Evaluation

No RoA can be successfully put in place in a single trial. We have not yet completed our evaluation for this year, but we have done enough to enable us to have next year's record in place. What have we learned? First, that we should have programmed the time to be spent on tutorial discussion into the timetable more formally. It became too easy in a singularly pressured year for both staff and students to postpone the formative stages, without which it is impossible to put an RoA in place.

Second, we should have paid more attention to the first rule about software: if you can't find anything wrong with it yourself, the users will. We have had a bug which was not thoroughly ironed out and students have been discouraged by this. The problem centred on the different types of printers used and their compatibility with the program.

Third, one cannot plan for the unexpected. Most students in the past few years have not obtained teaching posts until June. This meant that at the start of the summer term it was reasonable to put in place an interim summative record of achievement. This year we had not anticipated that with the advent of local management of schools, many teaching posts for the following September would be advertised much earlier and about half our students would have posts by Easter. This led to a lack of incentive to make a thorough job of the record in the summer term since they could see no immediate point in completing it.

The students, however, thought the idea a good one. They found it difficult to generate a style of writing which was appropriate to the record because of the division between the formative aspects and the need to produce a document which could be used in job applications. They felt that the work was particularly useful for self-appraisal, and some felt the broad headings were helpful for this. They felt too that it would be useful as a concrete record of what they had achieved; often this is quite difficult after one has completed the year's work. There were initial problems, but these disappeared through the year, and it was more use than they had expected at the start. They liked being able to write down positive comments, and felt that these were useful evidence and not bragging. The need to organize tutor time to complete the final production was confirmed, and we are taking action on this. It was useful, too, in giving experience of what pupils in school face in producing an RoA and it could also be used verbally at interview as an experience relevant to their future jobs.

For the coming year we have decided to change the direction of our RoA. It will now be called a 'record of personal development', and the emphasis will be on its role in appraising students' work during the course and helping them to formulate their goals for the next period. Each group of students will have a record planned for that group, though some groups will be retaining the record we already have. These latter groups will still be able to use the computer-based record, since the problems of printing will be less important with the change in objectives. In essence we tried to move too fast, and did not take sufficient account of individual differences in aims among members of staff. We have now agreed to move more slowly towards a common record. Part of the problem was that as a funded project there was pressure to have something in place in too short a time span. However, we have learned a great deal, and we believe that it will be easier to complete the processes more effectively during the next academic year.

The higher education dimension

Our approach has, however, a number of advantages which departments might like to consider in planning their own records. First, we have reduced the administrative cost of introducing such a record by virtually cutting out the need for secretarial staff to be involved in the detail of the work. This applies whether we use the computer-based approach or not. Second, we have increased the effectiveness of tutorial advice for students by programming into their work much of the informal advice which already took place and making sure that it really did happen rather than merely assuming that it would. Third, we are providing students with skills and documentation which are valuable in the preparation of future job applications.

The additional length of undergraduate courses will be a problem. It might be necessary to extend the document or to provide interim documents of a slightly different nature for each of the first two years of the course. This could be done with little difficulty, but it will demand effort to set it up in the first place. On the other hand, the longer course would allow for a much more considered document to be developed over several years, and personal input from tutors would be far more mature. Other problems are the lack of a clear vocational input for many undergraduate students until late in the course, and of staff acceptance of a scheme such as this one (it is pointless to impose a scheme which is not supported by staff). On the other hand, if a scheme has to be imposed, one which creates the smallest possible bureaucracy in order to put it into effect has clear advantages for us all.

References

1. Conferences Proceedings (1990) *Building the Bridge: Profiling the student teacher. Proceedings of a conference held at York 26–27 January 1990*, School of Education, Lancaster University, Lancaster.
2. Pritchard, K J, Jones, J P M and Loveluck, G D (1991) *Proceedings of the Conference on Record of Achievement in Initial Teacher Education*, School of Education, University of Wales, Bangor.
3. Pritchard, K J and Jones, J P M (forthcoming) *Proceedings of the Conference on Records of Achievement*, School of Education, University of Wales, Bangor.
4. Selkirk, K and Shipstone, D (1991) *Records of Achievement: a staff development workshop*, Nottingham University School of Education TVEI in Initial Teacher Training Project, Nottingham.
5. DES (1990) *Records of Achievement: Circular No 8/90*, Department of Education and Science, London.
6. DES/WO (1989) *Records of Achievement: Report of the Records of Achievement National Steering Committee*, Department of Education and Science/Welsh Office, London.
7. Selkirk, K E (forthcoming) 'A record of achievement for a Post-Graduate Certificate in Education Course', in Pritchard, K J and Jones, J P M (eds) *Proceedings of the Conference on Records of Achievement*, School of Education, University of Wales, Bangor.

Chapter Seventeen

Diploma of Personal and Professional Development

Helen C Gladstone

Introduction

Brunel University has until now run all its courses on the thin sandwich structure, by which students alternate six months of academic study with six months of work experience, ending with a fourth year of three terms in the university. There is general recognition of the great value to students of supervised work associated with their discipline areas. By the third period of work experience, students generally undertake work at very responsible levels. They demonstrate the maturity of outlook built up from the experience of applying their academic knowledge in real economic settings. Courses are designed to integrate work experience and academic study by setting employer-generated project work into the curriculum for each year of the courses, and by requiring students to undertake assessed distance learning assignments while they are remote from the university on work placement.

So what's new?

Along with many other institutions, Brunel is having to admit many more students. To do so, it has introduced three-year straight academic options for those in a hurry, like overseas students, or those financing themselves. It has also introduced four-year thick sandwich courses, by which students can spend one continuous year on work experience before entering the fourth year. The supervised work experience element is a feature of Brunel education, and the university wants to retain the sandwich principle, so far as practicable, as its premier educational offering. It has proved its value.

One benefit of sandwich education is that it allows students an opportunity to decide what type of work they will find most congenial. Employers welcome graduates who have this maturity. Brunel demonstrates the value employers place on sandwich courses by consistently coming top of the employment of graduates statistics.

To continue to attract students to apply for four-year courses, when they could opt for the quicker academic-only experience, Brunel has decided to mark their four-year courses with distinctive value. The university will record the achievements of students on work placements, monitoring and assessing these, and award a classified diploma at the end of the process, in addition to the classified degree.

In a less than totally motivated society, students' approaches to how much work they do are governed by what they get for their efforts. The award of a diploma motivates them to sustain their study discipline in their work placements, and to make more effective use of these privileged opportunities, in work environments protected by workplace supervisors and visiting tutors.

The proposal

Brunel uses the learning contract approach to make students aware of how much they can achieve during work placements, and to set definite objectives to be achieved. With tutorial guidance, they draw up personal learning objectives, before they leave the university. These include some specific and some general skills:

- details of study assignment(s) set by departments;
- details of anticipated acquisition of professional knowledge;
- details of anticipated acquisition of personal skills:
  - self-management and development
  - managing tasks
  - communicating in writing and speaking
  - working with and relating to others
  - applying course knowledge
  - applying initiative in work problems.

At the start of placements, students show their learning objectives to their supervisors, and make such modifications as fit their aims to workplace requirements. They then negotiate with their supervisors a programme of work to meet the learning aims and the needs of their employers. I make no apology for imposing this obligation on students, since negotiating towards mutual satisfaction is a skill which they will need throughout life. The interests of students and employers are expected to coincide in a sharper focus on what can be achieved. Students set a timescale against items listed on their programmes of work. These two sections form the learning plan, which students go ahead and implement under the guidance of their workplace supervisors.

Students are alerted to the likelihood that learning plans will not fall into place as anticipated. They are told that they will gain credit for sensible responses to whatever contingencies arise. After all, they are training to be professionals, on whose responses employers can depend. There will be one and probably two tutorial visits by Brunel academic staff during a six months' placement, to give tutorial guidance to students and to mediate between students and supervisors. Tutorial checks are made on students' regular self-assessment of their progress against the objectives set.

Previously, many departments did not assess students' activities on work placement, because of the worry of comparing performance in a 'good' placement dedicated to training, with performance in an unsupportive environment. This meant that students received no credit for working well beyond the permission to proceed. That was a pity, because it was demotivating, and many academically mediocre students redeemed themselves by revealing talents for workplace skills. The learning contract approach means that there will be much greater commonality of opportunity to learn. Workplace supervisors and academic tutors will not simply assess what students are doing for their employers, and whether they complete responsible or trivial tasks. Rather, they will assess what students are learning against the criteria set in their learning plans: it is the amount of learning which we are assessing. The learning plan provides a means of allowing for differences in employer support. Students can use experience of small firms just as easily to develop self-management skills, initiative and communication skills.

This new approach requires students to be much more aware of how they relate to the permanent staff in the workplace, and how well they interact with employees to solve problems. It encourages reflection on what students are doing or, in current educational terminology, 'deep learning'. Students are asked to keep records of their own perceptions of how they are doing in relation to their objectives. The development of students' judgements on how well they are doing – self-knowledge – is a key benefit. As well as students' self-appraisal, workplace supervisors are encouraged to write their comments under headings of:

- quality of work during placement;
- quality of personal relations with other staff;
- suggestions for actions which could lead to a better performance, or better understanding of life in the workplace.

Supervisors are specifically asked not to grade students' performance, because in general they have too few students on placement to define standards.

At the start of the new academic year, tutors will consider the students' own records, their tutorial visit notes, employers' comments, and grade performance on a scale from fail to pass with distinction. Tutors will be assessing things like:

- departmental assignment(s);
- development of personal skills;
- quality of students' records/logbooks/portfolios;

- understanding of the workplace.

Accumulating over the years at university, students' RoAs in supervised work experience will be quality controlled documents, which will be the product of the students' own tutored judgements on accomplishments, monitored by workplace supervisors and academic tutors. The reward will be the classified Diploma in Personal and Professional Development. We are trying to link this into national accreditation schemes. The outcomes will be young people who are better prepared to meet the expectations which employers have of modern graduates.

Implementation

So far I have outlined the Brunel situation and the scheme. I should state that discussions had been taking place towards introducing a more formal structure to work experience, its assessment and recording, for good educational reasons, before it became a selling point for the four-year courses.

Now I shall relate some of the difficulties associated with implementing the Brunel scheme. The scheme was approved by senate in March 1992, just in time for the unsuspecting students to be told of this new structure to their work experience when they departed at the end of March for placements all over the country. So far as is known from slight evidence, the students were enthusiastic about the Diploma. They were eager to accumulate evidence of how well they performed in the workplace. A difficulty for the students was the need for them to negotiate a programme of work with their employers. The term 'negotiate' seems to have acquired negative overtones. The students felt that they simply had to work at whatever they were told to do. They found it difficult to believe what employers had told us: that they welcomed a structure on which to plan work for students. We need to prepare students before they leave Brunel, to discuss work in terms intended to produce agreement with their employers.

The staff had a number of areas of concern, mainly arising from misgivings relating to fair assessment. Although discussions had been going on in the university for some time, the decision to go ahead with the scheme at senate left the majority of staff little time (two weeks) to absorb the ideas. A staff workshop was provided to familiarize staff with the concepts, at which an employer assured them of the benefits, but we need to provide further opportunities for staff to debate the issues. Staff saw the need for them to help each of their tutees prepare learning objectives, and are guiding students through the experimental first run. We are still discussing levels of achievement for the grades of 'satisfactory' and 'pass with distinction' of the Diploma.

The message here is to plan for a long run-in period if possible. We decided that it was better to experiment this year, with only some staff committed to the scheme, than have the students lose another year while staff came round to the idea. Some departments adopted the scheme immediately. The special engineering programme, Brunel manufacturing engineering, electrical engineering, materials technology, physics, biology and biochemistry, and computer science are running pilot versions with their own small variants to the model with their second-year students. These students will be eligible for the Diploma when they graduate in 1994.

Brunel staff have a long established supervisory role in work placements and pay tutorial visits to students. I am optimistic that experience will show staff that the Diploma will not require extra work, but more focused and more rewarding work with students who are aware of the added value to their personal and professional development. This is the intention conveyed in the title we have chosen for our Diploma of Personal and Professional Development.

SECTION 5:
Records of Achievement and Learning in Employment

Introduction

The process of transfer from higher education to employment is enhanced by the use of a Record of Achievement. It is further enhanced when there is continuity of emphasis, as illustrated in the chapters presented next, where employers emphasize the RoA as a powerful developmental model rather than a narrow mechanistic one.

Profiling provides an invaluable means of recording an individual's learning on work placement. As Sue Drew and Keith Willis point out in their chapter in this section, there is an emphasis, nationally, on promoting the accreditation of work-based learning. Even if no formal accreditation is afforded, the benefits to students are enormous, in that they are required to take responsibility for negotiating their learning contract with their work place supervisor, keeping a weekly log and producing reports for the workplace supervisor and visiting tutor. These processes give students the real-life opportunity to reflect their learning in the workplace, to review it, to formulate realistic action plans and to record their achievement 'in a physically demanding, potentially hazardous and tough environment' as one contributor puts it.

Nigel Smalls' account echoes a perceived need to empower the individual and relates how a major company is attempting to develop a culture which promotes self-development and self-awareness in its managers. He sees the NRA as being a powerful tool in helping business to recruit people with such experience and helping the individual to gain job satisfaction.

Another employer, Danny Moy, also strongly endorses the importance of empowering individuals to take responsibility for their own learning beyond formal education, through a variety of learning opportunities. As part of his work for the Records of Achievement National Steering Committee (RANSC) he was impressed by the ways in which the RoA philosophy enhanced the self-esteem of students and involved them in planning their own futures, something which his company (Argos) is attempting with its staff.

Finally, Rob Bellis identifies three key reasons for promoting RoAs at KMPG Peat Marwick. These are again primarily concerned with the development of the individual, through the process of self-analysis and feedback.

Chapter Eighteen

Recording Learning and Development on Sandwich Placements

Sue Drew and Keith Willis

BEng civil engineering: the context

During placement, many civil engineering students work on construction sites, far from the office situation familiar to most professional staff, in a physically demanding, potentially hazardous and tough environment, where quality, deadlines and costs are of paramount importance. On placement, students will be involved with both practical skills, working with complex and unfamiliar equipment, and with management and 'people' skills, working in teams being crucial. The learning potential is enormous.

In September 1991 the Personal Skills and Qualities project of Sheffield City Polytechnic (as it was then) was commissioned by the institution's school of construction to help develop a scheme to better enable the identification of students' learning on placement, initially working with the BEng civil engineering course which has a one-year industrial placement. The course has a very good reputation with employers and a well-established placement scheme. The impetuses for reconsidering the existing scheme included:

- a need, given the extra costs of sandwich courses, to justify the 'value-added' by placement;
- the institution's focus on the development of professional and personal skills and qualities (PSQ), eg, communication or interpersonal skills, problem solving, using initiative, being persistent, etc.;

- a growing general interest in attaching credit to placements (relevant initiatives include CATS, NCVQ, competence-based assessment and APEL).

One of the challenges was to create a scheme which might provide support and an opportunity for reflection, and which would better identify and record learning and development in a work context where immediate practical problem solving would usually have priority.

Consultation

Eight key members of academic staff and six employers (small/medium/large/public/private) were interviewed. Second- and final-year students were consulted in separate class sessions. The consultations revealed a variety of needs, for example, for clearer aims and structures; for improved support and feedback; for better preparation; for better clarification of students' motives; and for better identification of personal attributes and learning acquired. Constraints also emerged, for example: time and resource limitations; the workloads of both staff and students; the industry's susceptibility to economic recession and the consequent difficulties of finding placements and of pressure on those employers taking students; the variety of placements; and professional and awarding body requirements.

In the scheme developed, a student-drafted learning contract forms the basis for discussion between employer and student at interview. The contract is in two parts, with students specifying the learning outcomes they hope to obtain within two frameworks:

1. Relates to the Institution of Civil Engineers (ICE) core objectives. Where an employer already has a scheme using these core objectives, the students use that rather than the institution's. This caters for the fact that while some employers use elements of the ICE training scheme during placement, others do not.
2. A PSQ framework, based on BTEC's Common Skills, which all students use, irrespective of employers' systems.

Once offered a placement, the student carries out individual work and study to prepare for it. At the start of placement, possibly the first time when the student's actual job location is known, the student is responsible for discussing the learning contract with the workplace supervisor, revising and agreeing it. The contract can be amended as the situation changes, as it frequently does. The student is then responsible for setting up quarterly meetings with the workplace supervisor, and is visited twice during the year by an academic tutor.

The student, workplace supervisor and tutor all receive guidelines explaining the system and their respective roles and responsibilities. Additionally, the student has seven advice notes which explain each stage. During the second year, support will be built-in in the form of a conference where final-year students present their placement experiences to second years, two group sessions, and an individual tutorial.

Recording achievement

The student-produced documents recording achievement on placement are:

- the learning contract agreed (and amended) with the workplace supervisor (formative);
- a brief summary of preparatory work/study carried out (summative);
- a weekly logbook recording activities, successes, concerns, development, change, realizations (mainly formative);
- a summary of learning and development which refers to the learning contract and which goes in advance to the workplace supervisor and visiting tutor before review meetings (both formative and summative);
- a final technical report (summative);
- a final learning and development report, based on the learning contract, weekly log and summary sheets (summative).

These documents enable the student to reflect on learning and development, to plan action to build on strengths or work on weaknesses, and to record achievement. The previous scheme had some similar elements, but the new elements have a different focus – on personal growth and on outcomes, as well as upon the activities carried out and experience and knowledge gained.

Since the scheme mirrors many of the ICE requirements, it is hoped that students should subsequently be able to use the documents as evidence to contribute towards membership status. In addition to the student's records, the employer and tutor complete assessment sheets. At the moment, formal credit will not be attached to the placement year, but consideration is being given to students in future receiving an Industrial Placement Certificate.

The future

A small pilot is underway which involves seven BEng civil engineering students, six employers and four academic tutors over 1992/93. This pilot will be monitored and evaluated and recommendations will be made in the summer of 1993 about the scheme and its possible extension to all courses in the school in 1993/94. If the scheme is extended, other relevant professional bodies must be consulted, since courses in the school also prepare students for building and surveying careers, to check if the ICE part of the contract needs replacing by a framework appropriate for their requirements. Hopefully an advantage of the scheme is its flexibility in allowing differing frameworks to be used.

Academic staff are happy with the overall concept of the scheme but concerned about the amount of paperwork involved and whether the scheme may be too time-consuming, particularly for employers. The students' feedback will be crucial in any revisions and in developing an effective scheme which fits both the ethos of the course and the industry and meets the needs of all concerned.

Chapter Nineteen

Self-Development –
The Buck Stops Here
Nigel Smalls

A provocative title deserves some explanation. It is my intention to show that there is a necessity to match more evenly the delivery of educational training in HEI to the needs of the employers, and that Courtaulds Textiles believes that the NRA can give us the opportunity to establish the measures that have been taken by individuals and their colleges to prepare them for employment.

Skills are more important

The principle behind this requirement is that we have found that the more successful we are at recruiting individuals with certain pre-defined skills, the better the performance achieved and the more likely the individual is to stay within the organization. Partly because we are a relatively non-technological business, but mostly because we are looking to pick up managerial talent from HE, we are actually less concerned with the vast knowledge gained, but rather in the abilities these individuals possess. We have taken on board research done by Klemp (1977, 1979, 1982) in the USA some time ago questioning the need for academic brilliance in management. This is not to say that we are not concerned with intellectual ability, but simply that we see this as a moving feast: the reason we go to HE is intellect, as it tells us that a threshold has been reached. We never make our offers conditional; if we have chosen well this will not be a problem as one of our criteria is that the individuals should be self-motivated to do their best. One point to clear up. Even in the technological roles we recruit for, we are still interested in the skills shown as these will reflect the sort of individual and how they would fit into our corporate culture.

Courtaulds Textiles

I would like to begin by telling the reader a little about the company. Courtaulds Textiles is a £900m turnover business mainly UK-based, covering all areas of the textile process; it is split up into around 50 pretty autonomous profit centres each with their own chief executive. At present there are approximately 17,000 UK-based employees and 5,000 others worldwide. We have interests in spinning; we are extremely strong in weft knitting, particularly stretch fabrics, and in lace, and we are also represented in the home furnishings markets. However, you are more likely to come across us as suppliers to Marks & Spencer, as car door panels in Rover cars, or seats on Nissan cars, or as brand names such as Aristoc, Berlei, Gossard, Wolsey, Lyle and Scott and Jockey. And of course, all well-heeled academics will know of Georges Rech!

Until 1990, we were part of the Courtaulds group of companies but were demerged quite against trends for enlarging businesses. The needs of the two sides were diverging dramatically: Courtaulds Textiles, a mainly UK-based retail supplier, and Courtaulds Chemicals, a multinational speciality chemical business. The capital requirements were staggeringly different: try arguing for a £4m new factory when the other directors want £200m for a chemical plant. As Sir Christopher Hogg predicted, the two companies separately have easily out-performed the market even in these difficult times and both are recognized by the City as tightly run, efficient organizations in their own industries.

Participation – the key

The cultures of the two businesses have moved apart since demerger. Courtaulds Textiles is particularly 'people-oriented' because in an industry which is generally mature, only superior commercial and managerial skill will help you to survive. We have identified, after quite a torrid time restructuring in the late 1980s up to the present, that the success of our business in competition across the world essentially lies in the superior performance of our people, and this means instilling in them the need to be more proactive in their participation and less accepting of the way their own jobs or careers are going. In terms of those on the shop floor, we are encouraging greater input, and we have gone as far as self-managed teams now being piloted in some plants.

Gaining participation is obviously a slow process because it means breaking moulds forged back in time, both in managers and subordinates, but it is happening and there is no doubt it will be successful. As employees become more educated they are more demanding and expectant. All we want to do is to say:

OK, so you want more say in what you do at work; in return we want you to take on responsibility for your own development; and no, don't come complaining that you aren't getting on; you prove that you can do more and then we'll see. No, we're not leaving you in the lurch: we will provide the environment and we will sometimes point you in the right direction, but we won't nursemaid you; your career path is determined primarily by you and not by us.

Self-development is frightening. Ask yourself this question: 'When did I look at myself completely objectively, and decide that what I need to do is improve myself?' I suspect there aren't too many of us who can claim truthfully to have done this. Yet this is in essence the culture we are trying to develop. One has a perception of one's own strengths and weaknesses, and at an appraisal may get one's boss' perception of the same, but how often does your colleague turn around and tell you what they really think about you? The reason is always the same: it is threatening and likely to cause offence.

Our competency approach – HPD

So, what do we do to combat this? Fundamental is a language of competency analysis we use to help with objectivity and a behavioural approach to managing performance. We use this in our recruitment, our appraisal systems, and in identifying the prime skills in a job so as to better match the individual to the job and develop them onwards for the next job.

Our language of competency analysis, called 'High Performance Development' or 'HPD' for short, is based on the work of the father of competency analysis, Dr David McClelland, who in the 1950s identified in his book, *Achievement Motivation*, that there were characteristics common to the behaviour of all successful people: athletes, managers and entrepreneurs. This work was extended over the years, especially by the American Management Institute (AMI), and 19 competences or groupings of skills were identified which related directly to successful managerial performance. This work was published by Richard Boyatzis in 1982 in *The Competent Manager*. In the late 1980s, this research was brought to the UK by Courtaulds and Frederick Patten was engaged to develop it for Courtaulds Textiles Group. He had been formerly the first head of leadership at the Industrial Society where he developed the action-centred leadership approach throughout industry. The language was Anglicized from the research, and three behaviours were carefully attached to each of the nineteen competences to explain further the essence of the competency, and these competences were grouped into five key management dimensions or clusters.

So it is easy to establish that here we have a sophisticated tool but it is how we have used it that makes it so powerful. It is being used to help our businesses to recruit and to move the right people to the right job; it is being used to assist in performance monitoring through a system of appraisal; and it is being used, partly through appraisals and in many other forms, to give direction to those seeking self-development.

The drive to self-development

The whole process of self-development was identified earlier as 'threatening' to some people: it suggests that someone isn't good enough at the moment, and this can lead to a feeling of insecurity. We have not solved this entirely, and there are some obstacles to this, particularly in a recessionary period where good individual performance doesn't guarantee a job, but a method of encouraging open, objective analysis of any individual's skills is extremely beneficial in gaining the total commitment to the process. And although the business gains from self-development, in reality the individual is the one who has most to gain, not just in terms of the added promotional chances, but also in the increase in job satisfaction.

Our idea of self-development is linked directly into the needs of the business. I recently went to visit one of our subsidiaries in France, where they have to spend 1.4 per cent of salary cost on training. Without a proper policy and method to talk about the training needs, the personnel function find themselves agreeing to some training needs which to them are crazy but which supposedly enhance the individual; it may have been my French, but I think I was told of a time when someone came asking for money to pay for training to play the castanets! Why? Because he hated his job. Now for me the need is to enhance the job, not provide incentives for training people to leave!

The process we use is as follows. We have instigated self-development workshops for young managers and for our first-line supervisors. These are identifiable groups willing to learn, and the process is applicable to any managerial level. We request these individuals, who are volunteers, to fill in a questionnaire which asks them to identify their own perceptions of their behaviour in certain situations. These questions are linked to the HPD competences, and a competency profile is created. The powerful part of the exercise is the identification of what others think of you. At the same time, the boss, two colleagues and three subordinates are asked by the individual to fill in the same questionnaire, and the results are averaged out as an alternative perception of strengths and weaknesses. This gives the manager areas to work on and follow-up workshops on a quarterly basis for a year help each one to understand their behavioural means to success. At the end of the period the questionnaires are filled in again and the 'shape' of the profiles is much closer. We see a need to spread this form of self-awareness across the business, but also feel that this identifying of strengths and weaknesses is an area where we could do with help from higher education.

Directive self-development

There is another vital method of setting about identifying the self-development needs of the individual and that is through open appraisal. We see appraisal as a forward- rather than a backward-looking event aimed at identifying ways of improving performance, unlocking potential, and an opportunity to improve the boss-jobholder relationship. In a much more simplified way than on the self-development workshops, managers and subordinates fill out an HPD profile of the person being appraised and this acts as a non-threatening introduction into topics for discussion relating to performance. Both sides are expected to bring evidence to the appraisal for special discussion where there is disagreement in perception of a competency. Both perceptions are noted and an agreement reached after discussion, where possible. Development plans are then drawn up to improve performance. A behaviourally-anchored rating scale has been devised to assist in selecting behavioural goals for individuals. I must stress that our appraisal system does not *rate* people, but merely looks to improve perceptions of performance in the belief that only practising behaviours will improve performance.

Coaching is the method we increasingly use to assist managers to help their subordinates achieve more and take on more responsibility for developing themselves. In all appraisal training and in teambuilding and 'leadership' courses, this form of 'empowerment' is being emphasized. Coaching can help the job holders to help themselves by reflecting back experience and making them think for themselves. Sometimes, though, the individual needs a training course or programme. To assist in this we have identified the major competences addressed by various courses and using the appraisal system can match training needs to the appropriate course. By doing this, we believe we can also make training more effective, especially with the use of follow-up reviews and distance learning.

RoAs and self-development

Where does the Record of Achievement fit in with our plans? I can best describe this by telling you of some of the things we have been doing in the graduate recruitment market. Using one of the tools of our competency language, we have been able to identify the seven major competences that we look for in a prospective candidate. We have also identified four contra-indicator competences, lack of evidence of which we would consider as being of concern. On the application form, questions have been devised to draw out evidence of these questions. In pre-selection and then in interviews, we are analysing suitability to match against our needs. This is all a process to try to match the individual to the job demands within the Courtaulds Textiles working environment. What we have found is very little evidence from many prospective employees that they understand what we need from them, or their own skills. They have almost always boned up on the company but know little about the job. They may have carried out plenty of activities without relating to the real reason behind their success or failure.

'Skills workshops' have recently been introduced instead of evening presentations, as well as production case studies, and 'how to be interviewed' sessions. Those attending have found the objectives to be fully realized and many have had their eyes opened. From our point of view, as employers, it has helped to filter out many otherwise unnecessary applications from people who as a result realize that they should be looking for a different career. For all those attending there is an opportunity to test their skills in the areas of, among others, organizing, delegating, planning and teamworking.

Our natural link in the thought process is to ask: why are we doing the identification and development of skills; why can't students be better placed to understand their own abilities earlier, and be developing those they want for when they will need them? With an RoA, properly verified and authorized, we as employers would have some of the evidence to make decisions on recruitment, and careers advisers would be better able to advise. More and more businesses are using some kind of profiling of what they need against which to match skills. There could be less waste of time on all sides. RoAs give individuals early recognition of their roles in identifying their strengths and weaknesses, and make them take responsibility at an early stage for the development of their careers. An RoA gives the holder the ability to better manage the portfolio of their career, to form the basis of something potentially more meaningful than a curriculum vitae. In a future labour market where more jobs will be contracted out, it could form as essential a part in the recruitment process as a designer's portfolio of work does at present.

Conclusion

So what of the future? To better match graduate candidates to our needs at a pre-employment stage means concentrating our efforts on fewer universities and on specific departments within them. Not that this means exclusively textiles departments, and it does not exclude applications from any other individual. Our idea is to become involved with first years to give them input on what their skills are now, what they are likely to need in employment, and how they might work towards achieving this by practising behaviours. Following these people through HE will give us and them a track record to work with; we will identify more suitable candidates and help others to move into other careers. For the proactive department, the candidates will become far more readily identified as part of that department, willing to be involved to improve their own skills and enhance job prospects. We currently have proposals out at two university departments for doing this.

Most importantly, though, we will inject the idea at the pre-employment stage that whereas up until then they as individuals have had few decisions to make about their life and direction, now self-development is the key that will open the door to opportunity, and that key is actually in their own hands.

References

Klemp, G O Jnr (1977) 'Three factors of success', in *Relating Work and Education*, Jossey-Bass, San Francisco.

Klemp, G O Jnr (1979) 'Defining, measuring and integrating competence', in *New Directions for Experiential Learning*, Jossey-Bass, San Francisco.

Klemp, G O Jnr (1982) *Assessing Pupil Potential: An Immodest Proposal*, McBev, Boston.

Chapter Twenty

Records of Achievement and Self-development: a Business Initiative in Argos

Danny Moy

Introduction

In July 1990 the board of directors of Argos Distributors Limited (ADL), the largest operating company within Argos plc, agreed to make a significant addition to its management development strategy. In October 1990 the running of a self-development workshop for a group of 15 senior managers marked the formal beginning of implementing the revised strategy.

The workshop was the start of a process designed to realign the partnership between the company and individual managers in formulating and meeting management development needs. In essence, the balance of responsibility was to be shifted significantly towards the individual, with the expectation that there would be a consequent redefinition of the form of continuing support required from the company. It was also foreseen that individuals would increasingly influence that redefinition.

This shift in strategy did *not* mean the abandonment of established traditional systems like appraisal and training courses, nor was it designed to accommodate only 'high flyers' or other élite groups, nor indeed, as some cynics suggested, was it to get management development on the cheap. The decision was taken with the same business aims in view as are relevant to all our decisions about the business: to add value currently and to promote the achievement of strategic goals into the future.

The decision to invest in self-development as a strategic initiative was based on the conclusion, after review, that what we were currently doing to promote and support management development was necessary but not sufficient to meet business needs into the future. Several factors contributed to this conclusion:

- The information base that we currently used to appoint, develop, train and promote people was fragile. It depended heavily on inputs from senior management and did not sufficiently represent the wealth of pertinent information available from the individual managers concerned. To improve on this, we needed more information, better information and shared information.
- To help provide this information, individual managers needed processes additional to those already provided to help them understand their own capabilities and limitations, their longer-term aspirations and the investment of time and energy that they were prepared to put into achieving them.
- There was also a need to meet the changing expectations that people bring to work, including the desire for more involvement in decision making about their own futures. We needed to reflect in our management development support systems the dynamism of our operating environment, characterized as it is by company growth, change and uncertainty.

Self-development in Argos: structure and process

The formal structure around which the Argos self-development initiative is built starts, as already indicated, with a self-development workshop. This residential programme is run over one evening and two days. The primary aim is to help delegates to understand the concept of self-development and to begin to work on identifying their own development needs.

It must be stressed that the workshop is only the beginning of a continuous process. It is not a traditional training course. It establishes the base of understanding on which the delegates are expected to build into the future. The continuing support offered by the company is described later, after the workshop process itself is dealt with in more detail in the next section.

Self-development workshop

The workshop is viewed as an opportunity for each delegate to consider the salient factors that influence career development and to begin to formulate a personal development plan. The process can be summarized as one of taking stock, analysing, clarifying, reflecting, reassessing, and short-term action planning.

The process ranges over a wide variety of issues, as illustrated in Figure 20.1.

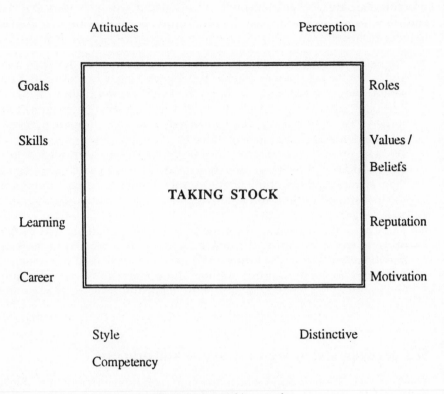

Figure 20.1 *Taking stock*

Attitudes and perception
We spend a deal of time in the earliest part of the workshop exploring attitudes and perceptions, dealing specifically with issues like positive and negative mind sets, in order to help delegates to understand more clearly how their own basic orientations towards success and failure can influence their personal development.

Roles and goals
A fundamental building block for self-development is the understanding of how congruent or otherwise one's life and career goals are with one's significant life roles. Consequently, we spend considerable time helping delegates to clarify the issues involved there.

Learning and achievements
Just as in the RoA, there is great emphasis on identifying and acknowledging personal achievements: what has been learnt so far, how one learnt the significant things and what is still to be learnt.

Identifying skills

A lot of time is devoted to identifying individual skills which can then be used to identify distinctive competences. The importance of distinctive competences is that they act as quite powerful 'career anchors', so defining and limiting suitable career paths.

Some concepts about career

Issues about career choice, stages and anchors are dealt with in some of the more formal aspects of the workshop because these are concepts that most delegates have not consciously dealt with before. The immediate aim of these inputs is to provide shared models and vocabulary for discussing the issues involved and applying them to each person's own circumstances.

What's helping? What's hindering?

At the action planning stage towards the end of the workshop, delegates are asked to identify factors within themselves and externally that will help or hinder in progressing their own development, and also ways of using these insights to go forward after the workshop.

Developing current job role

In looking at their own personal development plans (PDP) each person is advised to start with the current job role and reappraise its possibilities for personal development.

Action planning

In addition, they spend some time revisiting the action outputs they added to their personal planning sheet as they completed each phase of the workshop.

Getting started

Finally, they are advised to identify the first, perhaps small, steps to be taken within three days of leaving the workshop. This advice is based on the observation that good intentions tend to remain just good intentions if some relevant action is not taken within 72 hours of action planning.

Sustaining Momentum

Although one implication of self-development is that the overall balance of responsibility tips towards the individual manager, it would be naive to think that the initiative could be totally self-sustaining. Therefore, positive follow-up support is crucial if the potential benefits for the organization and the individual are to be realized. In summary, the continuing support process in Argos is based on the following activities.

Personal development plan

The self-development workbook introduced and used during the workshop serves as the basic record of the relevant data that will help to establish PDP and an implementation strategy for each delegate.

Individual follow-up meetings

As well as the normal post-workshop discussion with his or her nominating manager, each person who has completed a workshop is offered several one-to-one counselling meetings to help with the production of a PDP and its implementation. Typically these meetings take place three or four times a year.

Group follow-up meetings

The delegates from each workshop meet together with the workshop tutors in a follow-up session to review the effectiveness of the workshop and to check the progress made in establishing PDPs. This meeting takes place two months after the initial workshop. A further formal review meeting takes place 12 months after the workshop.

Managers as mentors

Further training has been introduced to help managers develop their skills as coaches, counsellors and mentors. One workshop was run in 1991, and further events are planned. The aim of this activity is to enable managers to carry out the bulk of support work for their own staff, and possibly in some cases as mentors for staff from other departments.

Further developmental opportunities

We are still in the process of agreeing how to build into our formal developmental system processes such as secondments, cross-functional job transfers and other non-training course solutions to agreed developmental needs.

Interim evaluation

At the end of July 1992 over 80 managers were at various stages of the self-development process within ADL. By the end of 1992 there were nearly 100.

A full formal evaluation of the initiative was completed by the end of the year. What can usefully be concluded about its value as a business investment? Some of the beneficial effects at the level of the individual manager can be summarized as follows:

- much greater clarity about, and ownership of, personal development issues;
- enhanced confidence in putting personal development issues on the agenda in discussions about work performance, potential for advancement, career aspirations, etc.;
- discovering the possibilities of the current job role for self-development;
- enlarged networks of personal contacts across the company, which are helping to broaden corporate knowledge and understanding;
- greater willingness to look beyond training courses to meet developmental needs;
- dealing more creatively with appraisal and coaching of staff, through applying some of the principles introduced in the workshop.

It is in the nature of a strategy like the Argos self-development initiative that the benefits to the business have to be tracked and evaluated over the longer term. Our formal evaluation, mentioned earlier, will begin that process.

In the meantime, we can say that the more informal evaluations carried out so far suggest that the main immediate corporate benefit is an increase in the participating managers' regard for the company and a consequent strengthening of their attachment to it as an organization with which to build a career.

Records of Achievement and Self-Development

In the Records of Achievement National Steering Committee (see Chapter 1) we spent a deal of time on the practical issues surrounding the document of record. Quite rightly so. If, for example, the document of record were seen as potentially useful in the job application process, it was absolutely right to ensure that it would be in a form that employers could use and that it would be available when school-leavers wished to use it for that purpose.

From my first exposure to RoA, however, I felt that the real importance of RoA was its informing philosophy and the developmental processes that it gave rise to: the emphasis on partnership, planned discussion, self-appraisal, self-management and taking increasing personal responsibility for one's own learning. The dynamism of the total process underlines the continuity of learning beyond formal education, and the variety of learning opportunities available.

When, some 20 years after leaving school teaching, I revisited schools as part of my work on RANSC, I was surprised and impressed by the changes I saw. It was not that everywhere I went everything was better than it had been in the early 1960s; far from it. It was rather that the issues being addressed and how they were being addressed pointed to some radical reappraisal of the educational process. It was difficult at the time, with so many initiatives being introduced into schools, to disentangle exact cause and effect of all these changes. It did seem to me, however, that the RoA initiative was right at the centre of the positive changes. Much of what I found appealing was to do with the enhanced self-esteem of students and the sense of involvement in their own futures that the best RoA practice was promoting.

The other development that struck a chord with me as a business manager was the changing role of the teachers. Just as managers within a self-development culture have to become skilled in the full range of mentoring skills, so educators have had to develop their own role concepts beyond the more directive activities of teaching, assessing and examining.

Chapter Twenty-one

Why Use Records of Achievement? An Employer's Perspective
Rob Bellis

The KPMG experience

I would like to tell you something of the KPMG experience in managing personal development and career planning and suggest some key reasons for the continued promotion of RoAs.

Some five years ago I accepted an invitation to join the graduate recruitment team. It took just a few months for me to realize how rewarding the challenges were and I was duly re-sprayed as a personnel professional. I work particularly closely with the UK training manager and his team in ensuring that the students we recruit are effectively trained, developed and managed over the three years of their training contract. In addition, I have been especially pleased to join the firm because it has been involved with personal skills development and Enterprise in Higher Education (EHE) since its inception. KPMG views personal skills development and EHE very seriously. My team takes part in numerous skills programmes throughout the year at schools and universities with students and teachers, as well as being involved in KPMG's internal skills courses.

In KPMG, the chartered accountants' institutes provide a regulatory framework for the pre-qualifying student. The training record of the Institute of Chartered Accountants in England and Wales (ICAEW), and the log book of the Institute of Chartered Accountants in Scotland (ISAS), for example, are the 'Records of Achievement' which are scrutinized before a student accountant can be admitted to membership. The requirements here are similar to those you would find for engineers and other accountancy bodies.

Careers development programme

Many view chartered accountants as the dull and boring, grey-suited individuals satirised by John Cleese in the Monty Python series. The reality is starkly different. Clients have become ever more demanding and it is simply not acceptable to be only technically proficient. Over the years, an increasingly sophisticated programme of personal skills development courses has evolved. To match this, two years ago the firm introduced an enhanced careers development programme. It was designed to encourage staff, early on in their careers, to think about how they are developing professionally and personally, about the sort of things they find most satisfying and what sort of work they might like to be doing in the future. This, in turn, will help determine the skills they ought to be developing and the training and experience they should seek in order to be properly equipped to handle that work and make informed career decisions.

In developing the programme, research was undertaken by the firm's human resources consultants to establish the skills which staff should develop and the opportunities available to them. The firm stresses the importance of counselling in helping individuals develop their own careers and in matching skills with opportunities. Two publications were introduced to support the programme: the Career Planner and the Career Development Guide. The Career Planner is essentially a personal workbook which assists staff in monitoring how they are developing. It is designed to be used for five years so that it extends for two years after the completion of the training contract. It can, however, easily be used for later career development and staff are being encouraged to use it in that way. The Career Planner should be completed by the individual in order to identify points concerning personal, short- and long-term development, for discussion at the regular appraisal and counselling sessions. It helps ensure a thoughtful and carefully planned approach to career development. The Career Development Guide is intended to simply lead the individual through the process.

The majority of employees do not take easily to reflection and self-analysis and view with some suspicion the formality of the career planner document; we had assumed that the 'new age' graduates were more advanced in self-assessment, promotion and development than was in fact the case. Some graduates certainly are more advanced in these ways: they are a joy to interview, they are harder to recruit and are more rewarding to manage and use this programme to good effect. They have probably already been on some formal skills programme at their place of higher education, be it an EHE, Student Industrial Society or departmental programme. It might interest you to know that in KPMG (London) last year, 30 per cent of the graduates taken on had graduated prior to 1991. This year the figure may be as high as 40 per cent and this is not just those taking a year out to 'find themselves' in Australia, Kenya, South America or New Zealand. Some of them are on worthwhile Operation Raleigh or VSO programmes, but at least half of them have begun their careers elsewhere.

We had expected graduates to want to be responsible and accountable for the way in which their careers are managed. Many are not ready for this. So, to prepare them to use our material and in order to support the excellent work of careers advisers around the country, KPMG have co-sponsored with ICI a career planner called 'Know Yourself, Know Your Future', prepared by members of the Association of Graduate Careers Advisory Services (AGCAS). One of my fellow managers was responsible for assisting Sue MacDonald, of Strategic Resourcing, in compiling and field testing this booklet that helps students undertake a personal brainstorming by focusing on what they have learned from past experiences, looking at what they are good at and what they enjoy. It should help them prepare for questions posed by employers on what they have done, how they have done it, what gave them the most satisfaction and how this influences the choices they will make.

Why RoAs?

So far as KPMG is concerned, there are three key reasons for promoting RoAs:

- To familiarize every individual, as early as possible in their career, with the process of self-analysis and feedback. This process is addictive once it has been used successfully.
- Within the accountancy profession, there has been a move towards case study examinations and competence-led assessments are on the horizon. Traditional and conventional methods of assessing individuals' talents and capabilities will be replaced. The professions' obsessions with 'O' and 'A' Level and degree classification may require a major overhaul.
- KPMG's personal and management skills courses are being delivered ever earlier on our graduate management programme.

Around 50 years ago, a 13 year-old girl wrote this in her diary:

Our examination results were announced in the Jewish Theatre last Friday. I couldn't have hoped for better. My report is not bad at all. They were certainly pleased at home, although over the question of marks my parents are quite different from most. They don't care a bit whether my reports are good or bad as long as I'm happy and not too cheeky: Then the rest will come by itself. I'm just the opposite, I don't want to be a bad pupil.. . .

Those of you familiar with the Diary of Anne Frank, will know what a fine and moving record of achievement it is.

Reference

The Diary of Anne Frank, Pan Books, London.

Part Three:
The Future

Chapter Twenty-two

The Future Role of Recording Achievement

Alison Assiter and Eileen Shaw

The book so far has indicated, we hope, some of the many advantages of profiling or recording achievement. The process has, however, not been without its critics. In this final chapter, we discuss some of these criticisms and some reservations which have been expressed about the value of the process. We begin by reminding the reader that there are at least two different purposes for which profiles may be used.

Types of profile

Personal or professional development profiles

One possible purpose of a process of profiling and recording achievement is to encourage in the individual owner a spirit of reflection on experience, goal setting and the recording of achievements. Some advocates of the NRA see this to be its primary purpose: the NRA should be seen, they say, as a document that sets in train a process of reflection and reviewing that continues throughout one's life. It does not stop when the school pupil leaves the school gates, or when the HE student moves into employment. It is, they say, designed to encourage a lifelong reflection on one's activities and lifelong learning. A profile which is used in this way, in the HE context, is a personal or professional development profile.

Personal development profiles are student-owned; they are not used formally in the assessment process. They involve individuals rating themselves as possessing, or not, particular skills. For example, at the University College of Ripon & York St John, students on humanities programmes rate themselves on a scale from 1–4 as possessing 'strong ability' or 'no experience at all' in a number of skills: writing, talking, arguing, researching.[1] Personal development profiles can be used to encourage self-reflection, self-awareness and self-confidence. Additionally, they can aid in the process of career planning. At Ripon & York St John, personal development profiles are linked in with a unit of the course that is run by the careers service, which is designed to help students make realistic choices about possible fields of employment. Several of the workplace profiles in this book are designed to help an individual make reasonable choices about future development in that workplace. Major national and international companies – Digital, IBM, Rover, to name but three – use profiling as part of their staff development and staff training programmes.

'Learning outcome' profiles used in assessment or accreditation

A profile with a different purpose is one that is designed for use in a programme of learning. Profiles used in this domain involve the setting of programme objectives in 'learning outcome' terms.[2] Learning outcomes are descriptions of what a person is able to do at the end of a programme of learning. Learning outcome profiles may be used either for a component or a module of a programme – a unit of a CAT system, for example – or for the programme as a whole. The unit itself might be based in an academic institution, or it could be the result of a process of prior learning, or it might be based in the workplace.

A 'learning outcome' profile can be deployed in two possible ways. First, it can take the form of a 'learning contract', where intended learning outcomes for the programme and agreed forms of evidence for the attainment of those are set. Second, it can fulfil the role of a summative record that documents the attainment of those outcomes and outlines the process of accreditation or assessment that has been used. The 'intended outcomes', in turn, can be either prescribed in advance (by tutor or workplace mentor) or they can be negotiated by the student in consultation with one of the former parties. The 'competency' model advocated by the NCVQ is one type of prescribed learning outcome profile.

These two separate motivational aims can be seen in the recording achievement process in schools where, in the 1970s, the focus was quite clearly on the process of individual target setting, recording and reviewing: the process of profiling. In the late 1980s, as the preparatory work for the NRA began to be undertaken, it is argued that the focus shifted onto the RoA as a document of record, that requires verification, and that the individual can use as a means of entry into FE, HE or employment. In this case, individuals must provide independent evidence for the claims they make on their records of achievement.

We would argue that both purposes are legitimate but that they are distinct. If they are conflated or confused with one another, then the potential disadvantages of profiling may outweigh the advantages.

Issues

Critical points

'Panopticism'

There have been 'in principle' objections to profiling, particularly as applied in the area of personal development. It has been argued that it is intrusive; that it is tantamount to a system of personal surveillance; that it is potentially punitive and debilitating. As one commentator[3] has put it:

We have to face and grapple with at least two important dilemmas of purpose and orientation that are bound up with this important innovation: dilemmas of motivation versus selection and independence versus surveillance.

Hargreaves argues that there are two opposing tendencies implicit in the profiling movement: tendencies to develop independence and initiative on the one hand, and towards instituting an insidious system of surveillance on the other. Profiling sets out to recognize and realize students' capacities and qualities – to foster and develop individual autonomy. However, there is a danger that it is doing precisely the opposite: that it is fostering a sophisticated system of social surveillance. Hargreaves refers to Foucault's appropriation of Bentham's 'panopticon' – a device for surveying prisoners without them seeing the warder – and Foucault's development of the expression 'panopticism', a principle of discipline in which power is exercised 'through an all-seeing but unseen observer'.[4] The power of panopticism resides not simply in observation, but in those being observed not knowing whether they are being seen at any particular moment. Because they are never sure whether they are being observed, prisoners become their own guardians. Hargreaves suggests that the 'progressive primary school' which uses profiling and where more and more aspects of a pupil's behaviour are subject to assessment, may tend in this direction.

There are several claims implicit in this. First of all, the critique is a general indictment of the profiling process, as tending to encourage a system of self-surveillance. Individuals are constantly advised to assess themselves, rate themselves, critically evaluate their performance. Sometimes, the critical point would then be, individuals ought to be free from this kind of process. But there may be at least two further kinds of criticism implicit in the Foucauldian/Benthamite metaphor. One is that the critical evaluation, encouraged by profiling, far from being potentially liberating, is in fact a subtle means of encouraging individuals to internalize possibly regressive social norms. Whatever values the major employers or some other powerful group happen to want individuals to acquire, are imbibed through the profiling process. But, the critic may continue, those values may not be the best ones for individual creativity and autonomy. Third, and finally, implicit in the Foucauldian metaphor is the point that some areas of personal experience ought to remain outside the domain of assessment – whether by oneself, one's peers or by authority figures.

The critical arguments are very important and illustrate the need for profiling to be seen to be a positive, student- or learner-owned, process. As soon as it is connected with a potentially punishing all-seeing retributive agent, its positive value disappears. Once it is associated with systems of reward and punishment that concern the 'whole' person, as opposed to one particular area of skill, then it may become a negative process, with the danger of social coercion. Thus it should neither be deployed to cover all conceivable aspects of personal development nor should it be used in a punitive fashion. As long as these points are kept in view, the negative implications are less likely to be felt and the danger of developing a record of incompetence can be reduced.

Advocates of profiling must keep in view the dangers of over-assessment and restrict the operation of the profiling process accordingly. Contrary to Hargreaves, however, profiling does allow for a number of different 'social norms' to be internalized or developed. The profiling process encourages in an individual the development of skills and qualities that foster an 'independent' approach to knowledge, as opposed to relying on authorities like the teacher, the school or a particular text.

Maslow

There is a related type of critical comment that may be made of profiling which involves looking at the intellectual roots of the profiling process. These roots lie partly in the humanistic psychology of Abraham Maslow[5] and Carl Rogers[6].

Profiling encourages individuals to develop their potential for autonomy and for self-directed behaviour. As we have pointed out, many in the EHE and capability movements emphasize self-development, critical self-appraisal and self-directed learning. Similarly, a key concept in Maslow's theory is 'self-actualization'. In his view, human needs exist in a hierarchy; the lowest are needs for food and shelter; once these are adequately gratified, 'higher' needs come into play; these are needs for 'self-actualisa-tion' – the realizing of one's inner potential. Like 'capable' people, 'self-actualizing' individuals are independent; they blossom to the extent that they are removed from dependency on others.

Some critics have, however, seen Maslow as the paradigmatic liberal individualist: they have argued that he advocates self-interest at the expense of the social origins of the self and the social context of behaviour.

Maslow, himself, went so far as to imply that full human liberation – from social inequalities and social injustices – could come about through a process of individual self-help. He viewed the process as a type of therapy. So far as we are aware, no advocate of profiling has made a claim of this profundity. We would argue, indeed, that profiling cannot in itself alter deep social inequalities or divisions. However, on the more positive side, profiling can help bring about some social change by altering individuals' perceptions of reality and then changing their behaviour: some employers who have hitherto accepted only Oxbridge graduates, for example, may come to recognize that very many other graduates possess the skills and capacities they require. Moreover, while profiling encourages autonomy and self-development, these skills can be fostered in students by, for example, working in groups with other students. Unlike Maslow, then, very many advocates of profiling attach considerable importance to the 'social context of behaviour'.

We would argue, further, that there is no particular reason to single out profiling as tending in the direction of surveillance, any more than assessment systems in general. In fact, learning outcome profiling tends to encourage a more open, more clear cut process of assessment, as distinct from the 'traditional' liberal humanist model in higher education which refers to the training of 'the powers of the mind'.[7] Traditional liberal humanist approaches to teaching, learning and assessment which are often imprecise about exactly what they are setting out to do, are more liable to tend towards an insidious system of control. In the case of profiling, students are more clearly aware of the aims and goals of any assessment process. Any 'control', therefore, is more open.

Profiling and deep learning
A further criticism of some types of learning outcome profiles is the following: there is proper scepticism of the potentially reductive implications of too rigid an application of the principle that students should have learning outcomes set for them. Some have argued that the principle militates against the 'deep learning'[8] that is the province of academic study at higher education level. There is some recent evidence, on the other hand, that this very deep learning may be facilitated by students knowing in advance, in more detail than has often hitherto been the case, what their learning targets are.[9] Knowing these targets enables students better to plan their learning; greater self-awareness about what a student is doing is likely to improve his or her performance. However, the point illustrates the need to think very carefully about what a learning outcome is. It could be a generic or transferable skill, for example.

Equal opportunities
There is a further issue that is implicit in some of the above criticisms of profiling; this concerns the equal opportunities dimension of the profiling process. Any profile which involves academic staff or employers outlining a list of skills against which students are to rate themselves must be concerned, as far as possible, with broad, generic skills, and not with those that are specific to a particular culture, race, sex or class. For example, 'communicates well' should not be interpreted as implying that the person speaks 'Queen's' English in the accent of the traditional white, civil servant. Of course, it is extremely difficult to ensure that any set of skills is not culturally biased in any of these ways, and it may be almost impossible to ensure that a white male, who is judging an Asian woman's self-assessment, for example, is not racially biased. However, an awareness of the potential issues is a step in the right direction. Many Asian women living in Britain would undoubtedly benefit, in employment terms, from a process

that encouraged them to rate themselves more highly in some of the qualities they require in order to 'succeed' in a white-dominated culture.

These are difficult and controversial issues. This equal opportunities question, indeed, is endemic in any kind of process which involves assessment, whether it be self-assessment or assessment by others.

Thus far, we have been outlining some of the critical comments which have been made about some or all types of profiling processes. In addition, there are some practical issues which arise for those interested in setting up a profiling system.

Practical issues

Using profiles in accreditation

One possible purpose of a profiling system, as we have already pointed out, is to provide a record of a person's achievements for external consumption: for an FE or HE institution or for an employer. Such a document will provide evidence that the person has achieved a certain level of knowledge or carried out certain tasks competently or effectively. What counts as evidence of such achievement and the appropriate sorts of check on the evidence are issues that will need to be resolved. There is an intuitive tendency, particularly where assessments are norm-referenced, to think that checks must be carried out by some third party. However, encouraging individuals to develop realistic self-assessments can be a tremendous benefit of profiling. There is no *a priori* reason why an external 'check' on a student or trainee's self-assessment should provide any greater guarantee of its reliability than the individual's own check, so long as the latter is conducted against some standard of achievement in the area.

Many of the issues that will arise are questions about assessment in general, and it is beyond the scope of this book to consider them in any detail or depth.

Quality assurance

There are, however, some quality assurance issues that relate to profiling in particular. Questions that may arise include the following: Was there a shared understanding of the meaning of profile elements? Where profiling involved assessment, for example of oral or presentational skills, were there checks on the accuracy of the grade of an individual marker? Was there a shared understanding of the grading criteria, in the case of graded profiles?

Many of these issues will be for individual or groups of academic tutors or workplace mentors; some of them in education, however, are strategic issues of concern to institutional managers. Institutional management will have to check whether the quality assurance procedures in place are appropriate for teaching and learning involving profiling. They will need to look, for example, at the role of external examiners; they will need to ensure that quality assurance mechanisms – annual reports, Academic Standards Committees, etc. – encourage course teams to refocus their programmes in the direction implied by profiling systems. In the end, institutional managers may have to move towards rethinking institutional teaching and learning strategies, so that some teachers take on a role more akin to a facilitator of learning than a traditional lecturer.

Profiling and the graded degree

One final area that may be of concern, both to the institutional managers and to teachers/mentors themselves, is the implication of profiling and related developments for the graded degree structure. In a cogently argued piece, and reflecting much thinking within the profiling movement, Richard Winter[10] argues that the graded degree structure is inappropriate for the sorts of assessment – against a *criterion*, or standard, as opposed to norm-referencing – that profiling encourages. This is an area which will, no doubt, be hotly debated in the next few years.

Resources

One of the concerns which has been expressed about profiling is that it is resource-intensive as far as the production of documentation is concerned, primarily, in terms of time – staff time to prepare the documents, to engage in staff development, and time properly to implement the profiling process – to carry out personal tutorials and to go out on industrial visits.

An implication of this is that profiling cannot be an 'add on' to existing teaching, learning and assessment processes. It requires a change in approach to these matters. But this change enables the better performance of existing learning tasks. Profiling clarifies for the learners what the learning process is all about, and enables students to plan their learning. Learning, therefore, becomes more efficient and this can save time, both for the student and for the lecturer or the workplace mentor. Setting targets for learning enables existing resources to be redistributed. Learning may take place by other means than has often been the case in HE: by group work, by experiences acquired outside the university or college. In the context of work-based learning, as chapters in this book illustrate, profiling gives focus and point to the traditional workplace visit in so far as the visit gains a structured place in the student's programme of learning. More efficient visits may lead to fewer of them being necessary in the student's pro-gramme. Evidence from the schools sector demonstrated that giving greater responsibility to the student not only reduced the pressure on staff but enhanced the motivation of the students. Additionally, profiling facilitates the transition between one course or work setting and another. It can, therefore, save time at the interfaces between modules of courses, or between courses and workplaces.

However, an institution-wide adoption of a profiling system or systems must lead to the redistribution of resources. Profiling can facilitate a more student-centred approach to teaching and learning in a mass education system. However, it will only do this if less time than has hitherto been the case is spent on traditional approaches to teaching and learning. Indeed, it encourages a move away from traditional approaches to teaching and learning, and towards more independent learning. This has major policy implications for universities and colleges. Clearly, it also has major developmental implications: it will only be effectively introduced into academic programmes if students, staff and employers are educated on the benefits of the processes of recording and reviewing achievement.

Challenges for the future

The RoA movement emphasizes students' self-esteem and their ability to take control of their own lives and seeks to liberate, to empower, and to encourage learners to manage their own learning. The NCVQ is producing national guidelines, written by practitioners, for secondary schools, institutes of further and higher education, employers and government training schemes, on the National Record of Achievement. It is imperative that, when producing national guidelines, we do not lose sight of the *raison d'être* of the RoA movement. Guidelines must not be couched in terms that prescribe, intrude, coerce or control. They need to help students develop the confidence and the means for taking responsibility for their own personal, educational, professional and vocational development.

We stand poised at the advent of a monumental opportunity to empower students for life. The extent to which this is exploited or missed, used or abused, remains to be seen.

References

1. See Fenwick, A, Assiter, A and Nixon, N (1992) *Profiling in HE*, CNAA and TEED, London, p. 65.
2. See ibid. pp. 8–9.
3. Hargreaves, A (1986) *'Ideological record breakers?'*, in Broadfoot, P (ed.) *Profiles and Records of Achievement*, Holt, Sussex.
4. Ibid, Hargreaves, p. 217.
5. Maslow, A (1973) *The Farther Reaches of Human Nature*, Pelican, Harmondsworth, and *Motivation & Personality*, (1973) 2nd ed, Harper & Row, New York.
6. Rogers, C (1978) *Carl Rogers on Personal Power: Inner Strength and its Revolutionary Impact*, Constable, London.
7. Robbins, Lord (1963) *Higher Education: Report of the Committee*, London, HMSO, cmnd 2154.
8. Robbins, Lord (1963) *The Robbins Report on HE*, Report of the Committee, HMSO, London.
9. Davies, L (1990) *Experience-based Learning within the Curriculum*, CNAA, London.
10. Winter, R (1993) *'Education or grading: arguments for a non-subdivided honours degree' Studies in Higher Education*, summer.

INDEX

160